The Wise Path to Wealth:

Unleashing the Power Within to Transform Your Financial Destiny

Robert D. Rackers

1

Table of Contents

INTRODUCTION:

In the heart of a bustling city, where dreams and ambitions collide, a tale of resilience, self-discovery, and unwavering determination unfolds. Welcome to "The Wise Path to Wealth: Unleashing the Power Within to Transform Your Financial Destiny."

In this captivating journey, we follow the lives of three extraordinary individuals who find themselves at the crossroads of their financial journeys. Meet Emily, a talented artist struggling to make ends meet, searching for a way to turn her passion into a sustainable career. Then there's Alex, a young professional with dreams of financial independence, but caught in the clutches of debt and societal expectations. And lastly, David is a seasoned entrepreneur seeking to create lasting wealth while balancing the demands of his personal and professional life.

As their stories intertwine, they embark on a transformative quest, guided by a mysterious mentor named Professor Sullivan. Together, they navigate the labyrinthine world of finance, uncovering hidden secrets, and unlocking the power within themselves to overcome financial obstacles and achieve true wealth.

Through the pages of this book, you will be captivated by the trials and triumphs of our protagonists. You will witness the highs and lows, the victories and setbacks, and the unwavering spirit that propels them forward. As their paths converge, you will discover timeless wisdom, actionable strategies, and profound insights that will empower you to shape your financial destiny.

"The Wise Path to Wealth" is not just a story; it is a tapestry woven with themes of resilience, self-belief, and the pursuit of abundance. It delves into the complexities of personal finance, exploring budgeting, investing, and entrepreneurship while tackling the emotional and psychological aspects that shape our relationship with money.

Within these pages, you will find practical tools, step-by-step guidance, and thought-provoking exercises that will challenge you to dig deep and unearth your true financial potential. You will learn to harness the power of mindset shifts, embrace calculated risks, and leverage the untapped opportunities that surround you.

But this is not just a book; it is an invitation to embark on your quest for financial freedom. It is a call to action, urging you to confront your fears, take control of your finances, and build a life of abundance on your terms.

So, dear reader, are you ready to join Emily, Alex, and David on their transformative journey? Are you prepared to unlock the secrets of wealth creation and harness your inner potential? Open the pages of "The Wealth Seekers" and prepare to be inspired, motivated, and empowered.

The path to financial abundance awaits. The adventure begins now, and together, let's shape a future filled with prosperity and fulfillment.

• Welcome and the significance of monetary freedom

Welcome to a world where the shackles of financial limitations are shattered, and the doors of opportunity swing wide open. Welcome to a journey that transcends mere numbers and bank statements, where the pursuit of monetary freedom takes center stage. Welcome to a book that will change the way you think about wealth, success, and the boundless possibilities that await.

In the fast-paced, interconnected global economy, the concept of financial freedom has taken on new meaning. It is no longer just a lofty aspiration or a distant dream reserved for the fortunate few. It has become a necessity, a pursuit that empowers individuals to break free from the chains of financial dependency and create a life of autonomy, abundance, and fulfillment.

The significance of monetary freedom cannot be overstated. It is a catalyst for personal growth, a passport to self-discovery, and a means to unlock the full potential that lies within each of us. It grants us the power to shape our own destinies, to pursue our passions without the constraints of financial constraints, and to make a lasting impact on the world around us.

Monetary freedom is about more than just accumulating wealth. It is about gaining control over your financial life, having the freedom to make choices that align with your values and aspirations, and living a life of purpose and meaning. It is the ability to pursue your dreams, nurture your relationships, and contribute to causes that ignite your soul.

But achieving monetary freedom is not a stroke of luck or a distant mirage. It is a journey that requires intention, discipline, and a strategic approach. It is about mastering the art of budgeting, saving, and investing wisely. It is about understanding the principles of wealth creation, leveraging opportunities, and managing risks. It is about embracing a mindset of abundance, fostering financial literacy, and continuously expanding your knowledge.

In this book, we will embark on a transformative exploration of monetary freedom. We will delve into the strategies, principles, and tools that can help you break free from the constraints of financial mediocrity and embrace a life of abundance. We will demystify the complexities of personal finance, guiding you through the maze of investment options, tax strategies, and wealth preservation techniques.

But beyond the practical aspects, we will also delve into the emotional and psychological dimensions of monetary freedom. We will address the mindset shifts, the limiting beliefs, and the behavioral patterns that can hinder your progress. We will empower you to overcome financial obstacles, develop a healthy relationship with money, and cultivate the habits and disciplines necessary for long-term success.

Throughout this book, we will share real-life stories, insights from experts, and practical advice that can be applied to your unique circumstances. We will provide you with the tools, knowledge, and inspiration to take control of your financial destiny and create a life of freedom, purpose, and abundance.

So, dear reader, are you ready to embark on this transformative journey? Are you ready to break free from the limitations that have held you back and step into a world of unlimited possibilities? If so, then join us as we unravel the secrets of monetary freedom, and together, let's chart a course towards a future filled with abundance and fulfillment.

Welcome to a life of monetary freedom. The journey begins now

CHAPTER 1

Underpinnings of Monetary Autonomy

Money related independence, the capacity of a country to practice command over its financial strategy and cash plays had a critical impact in forming the worldwide economy since forever ago. From old civic establishments to the cutting edge time, the quest for financial independence has been a main impetus behind monetary strategies and systems utilized by countries around the world. This article investigates the verifiable advancement of financial independence, inspecting the different monetary hypotheses and practices that have molded this idea and examining its suggestions for the worldwide economy. Besides, we will dive into the advancement of money related independence over the long run and break down its application in various nations.

Old Developments and the Starting points of Financial Independence

The foundations of financial independence can be followed back to old civic establishments, where the improvement of money related frameworks assumed a vital part in working with exchange and monetary movement. In Mesopotamia, for example, the presentation of normalized units of trade, like silver shekels, considered more prominent productivity in business and worked with financial development. Likewise, in old China, the utilization of metal coins as a vehicle of trade encouraged monetary coordination and provincial turn of events.

Be that as it may, the idea of money related independence as we comprehend it today arose during the Renaissance time frame and acquired conspicuousness during the period of mercantilism. Mercantilist countries tried to amplify their financial influence by aggregating abundance through exchange excesses and keeping up with command over their monetary forms. This quest for financial independence permitted nations to safeguard homegrown ventures, control expansion, and state their monetary power.

The Ascent of Focal Banking and Financial Strategy

The foundation of national banks denoted a huge achievement in the improvement of money related independence. In the seventeenth 100 years, the making of the Bank of Britain presented the idea of a concentrated power liable for giving and controlling a country's money. National banks furnished states with the resources to manage cash supply, balance out trade rates, and impact loan costs, consequently applying command over money related approaches.

The twentieth century saw further headways in money related independence, with the reception of different monetary speculations and practices. The highest quality level, which fixed monetary forms to a proper measure of gold, won during the late nineteenth and mid twentieth hundreds of years. Nonetheless, the highest quality level's impediments became evident during seasons of financial emergency, as it limited state run administrations' capacity to invigorate their economies through money related strategy.

The Shift Towards Drifting Trade Rates and Financial Adaptability

The breakdown of the highest quality level and the rise of drifting trade rates during the twentieth century denoted a huge defining moment chasing money related independence. Drifting trade rates permitted monetary forms to change unreservedly because of market influences, allowing nations more noteworthy adaptability in dealing with their money related arrangements. This shift furnished policymakers with apparatuses to address monetary lopsided characteristics, for example, expansion or downturn, through changes in loan fees and conversion standard mediations.

The Improvement of Local Financial Associations

In ongoing many years, the quest for money related independence has taken new structures through the foundation of provincial financial associations. Models incorporate the European Association's reception of the euro and the development of the West African Financial Association. These associations intend to improve financial incorporation, work with exchange, and advance provincial steadiness by blending money related strategies and making a typical cash. Notwithstanding, the achievement and difficulties looked by territorial money related associations differ, with suggestions for financial independence and the general working of the worldwide economy.

Advantages and Disadvantages of Financial Independence

Financial independence offers a few expected benefits for countries. It permits nations to fit their financial strategies to address explicit homegrown difficulties, like expansion, joblessness, or conversion scale soundness. Financial independence likewise gives a way to safeguard against outside shocks and impacts, empowering nations to answer deftly to monetary variances.

Be that as it may, there are likewise disadvantages related with financial independence. Keeping an autonomous cash requires cautious administration and may open nations to money vacillations and speculative assaults

Also, extreme financial independence can prompt protectionist measures, cash wars, and exchange irregular characteristics, influencing worldwide monetary soundness.

Utilization of Money related Independence in Various Nations

Money related independence has been applied distinctively across nations, impacted by authentic, political, and financial elements. A few countries focus on conversion standard soundness and decide to fix their monetary forms to a stable unfamiliar currency or a bushel of monetary standards. Others decide on adaptable conversion scale systems to conform to market influences. The degree of money related independence can likewise shift, as certain nations give up control by embracing normal monetary standards or taking part in financial associations.

Concluding;
The authentic improvement of money related independence has formed the worldwide economy and affected monetary strategies of countries over the course of time. From antiquated civilizations to the advanced period, the quest for money related independence has driven financial procedures and molded financial frameworks. The foundation of national banks, the shift towards drifting trade rates, and the development of provincial financial associations have all added to the advancement of money related independence.

Understanding the ramifications of financial independence is pivotal for policymakers, business analysts, and people the same. While financial independence awards nations command over their money related approaches and takes into account fitted reactions to homegrown difficulties, it likewise presents dangers and moves that should be painstakingly made due. Accomplishing an ideal harmony between money related independence and worldwide monetary participation is pivotal for encouraging soundness, advancing financial development, and propelling the prosperity of countries.

By concentrating on the authentic advancement of money related independence, the different financial hypotheses and practices, and its application in various nations, we gain important bits of knowledge into the perplexing transaction between financial arrangement, monetary sway, and worldwide monetary elements. With this information, we can take a stab at more noteworthy grasping, participation, and development to explore the intricacies of the worldwide economy and shape a more prosperous future for all.

• Center standards and the force of saving and effective financial planning

In the realm of money, sticking to laid out guidelines is fundamental to guaranteeing successful monetary preparation and saving. The Middle norms, perceived worldwide as core values for monetary administration, assume a critical part in advancing straightforwardness, responsibility, and security. This exposition investigates the meaning of keeping Center guidelines for people and organizations, underscoring the potential advantages they offer. Also, we will examine the dangers related with not sticking to these principles and how they can be relieved.

Figuring out the Middle Norms

The Middle norms envelop a bunch of standards and rules that give a system to compelling monetary preparation and saving. These norms are intended to upgrade monetary navigation, further develop risk the board, and encourage long haul maintainability. They address different viewpoints, including monetary revealing, inner controls, moral lead, and hazard evaluation. By keeping these guidelines, people and organizations can make a strong starting point for their monetary undertakings.

Advantages of Sticking to Center Principles

1.Improved Straightforwardness and Responsibility:
Keeping Center guidelines advances straightforwardness in monetary announcing, guaranteeing that data is precise, dependable, and available. This straightforwardness cultivates trust among partners, like financial backers, loan bosses, and controllers, eventually reinforcing the standing of people and organizations. Besides, complying to these norms advances responsibility, as it lays out clear rules for monetary execution assessment and guarantees capable stewardship of assets.

2. Further developed Chance Administration:

Center norms accentuate powerful gamble evaluation and the board processes. By keeping these guidelines, people and organizations can distinguish and alleviate potential dangers. This proactive methodology empowers them to pursue informed choices, defend against monetary misfortunes, and safeguard their monetary prosperity. Sound gamble the board rehearses add to long haul steadiness and versatility, even despite financial vulnerabilities.

3. Ideal Monetary Preparation:

Center norms give a methodical system to monetary preparation, empowering people and organizations to define practical objectives, dispense assets effectively, and track progress. By observing these guidelines, people can foster thorough monetary plans that include planning, saving, effective money management, and obligation to the board. Essentially, organizations can concoct vital monetary courses of action that line up with their targets, prompting better asset designation and practical development.

4. **Admittance to Capital and Venture Valuable open doors**:

Sticking to Center principles upgrades the validity of people and organizations, making them more appealing to expected financial backers and loan specialists. Exhibiting consistency with these guidelines flags a guarantee to monetary uprightness and mindful administration rehearses. This, thus, improves the probability of getting funding, getting to capital business sectors, and opening venture valuable open doors.

5. **Moral Direct and Notoriety**:

The Middle norms underscore the moral way of behaving, stressing the significance of uprightness, genuineness, and decency in monetary dealings. By sticking to these norms, people and organizations show their obligation to moral leadership, which assists fabricating a positive standing and encourages trust among partners. A solid standing for monetary uprightness can open ways to joint efforts, organizations, and client steadfastness, improving long haul achievement.

Dangers of Not Keeping Place Guidelines and Relief Techniques

1. Monetary Blunder and Failures:
Neglecting to stick to Center guidelines can bring about poor monetary administration, prompting wasteful utilization of assets, monetary misfortunes, and botched open doors. To relieve these dangers, people and organizations ought to focus on instruction and preparation on monetary accepted procedures, utilize qualified experts, and lay out powerful inward controls.

2. **Administrative Resistance**:
Overlooking Center principles might bring about administrative rebelliousness, uncovering people and organizations to lawful and reputational gambles. To relieve this, people and organizations ought to remain informed about material guidelines, draw in legitimate advice if

necessary, and execute inner cycles to guarantee consistent with applicable monetary regulations and rules.

3. Expanded Monetary Weakness:

Forgetting to adhere to Center guidelines can leave people and organizations helpless against monetary shocks and financial slumps. Relief procedures incorporate structure crisis reserves, differentiating speculations, and routinely reevaluating monetary designs to adjust to evolving conditions.

4. Harm to Notoriety and Trust:

Rebelliousness with Center norms can discolor the standing of people and organizations, disintegrating trust among partners. To keep away from this, people and organizations ought to lay out a culture of straightforwardness, responsibility, and a moral way of behaving. They ought to likewise convey their obligation to Center guidelines to partners and participate in standard revealing and divulgence rehcarsals.

End

As per the Middle, principles are fundamental for successful monetary preparation and saving. These guidelines give a hearty structure that advances straightforwardness, responsibility, and capable monetary administration. By sticking to these norms, people and organizations can appreciate advantages like upgraded straightforwardness, further developed risk of the executives, ideal monetary preparation, admittance to capital, and the development of a solid standing. Alternately, not adhering to these guidelines can prompt monetary fumble, administrative resistance, expanded weakness, and harm to notoriety. People and organizations should focus on consistency with Center principles to moderate dangers, jump all over chances, and prepare for long haul monetary achievement.

CHAPTER 2

Dominating Your Cash Mentality

Dominating your cash mentality is a groundbreaking excursion that enables people to assume command over their monetary lives and accomplish enduring independence from the rat race. In this paper, we will investigate the significant effect of our mentality on our relationship with cash and how it can shape our monetary results. Drawing bits of knowledge from "The Basic Way to Abundance" by Robert D. Rackers, we will dive into the critical subjects of saving, effective financial planning, and living economically, and how these ideas can be applied to dominate our cash outlook.

I. The Influence of Saving:
Creating an Underpinning of Financial momentum

One of the most vital moves towards dominating your cash outlook is fostering a saving propensity. Rackers underlines the significance of saving persistently and reliably, regarding it as a non-debatable cost. He notes, "Setting aside cash is the hole between your pay and your spending. The more extensive the hole, the quicker your abundance will develop."

Rackers shares the tale of Mr. and Mrs. Smith, a couple who began saving right off the bat in their vocations. By making little yet steady commitments to their reserve funds, they had the option to collect significant savings over the long run. This model exhibits that paying little heed to pay level, saving is accessible for everybody.

II. Money management: Developing Abundance with a Drawn out Viewpoint

Putting is an urgent component in dominating your cash mentality. Rackers advocates for a straightforward and detached speculation approach, for example, putting resources into minimal expense file reserves. He features the force of accruing funds and the significance of remaining contributed for the long stretch.

To show the advantages of financial planning, Rackers presents the instance of Sarah, a youthful expert who began putting right off the bat in her profession. By reliably adding to her speculation portfolio and reinvesting profits, Sarah's abundance developed dramatically over the long run. This model exhibits the capability of effective money management to speed up abundance gathering and accomplish monetary autonomy.

III. Living Efficiently: Augmenting Assets for Ideal Riches

Living efficiently is one more basic Chapter of dominating your cash mentality. Rackers challenge the common culture of industrialism and urges perusers to take on a careful and deliberate way to deal with spending. He states, "Living economically implies being insightful with our cash, focusing on our spending on what gives us veritable pleasure and fulfillment."

Rackers shares the tale of John, who chose to scale down his way of life and embrace thriftiness. By decreasing his costs, John had the option to save a critical piece of his pay and contribute it shrewdly. Over the long run, he accomplished monetary autonomy and the opportunity to seek after his interests. This model shows the way that living economically can prompt a really satisfying life, unburdened by inordinate material belongings.

IV. Conquering Restricting Convictions: Moving to an Overflow Mentality

To genuinely dominate your cash attitude, conquering, restricting convictions and shifting to an overflow mindset is fundamental. Rackers investigates the mental chapters of cash and what our outlook means for our monetary decisions. He stresses the significance of appreciation, expressing, "When you center around what you have and feel a debt of gratitude, you'll find you want less and can appreciate life more."

Rackers shares the narrative of Emily, who grew up with a world view limited by fear and continually stressed over cash. Through self-awareness and self-reflection, Emily had the option to move her outlook to one of overflow. She started valuing the basic delights throughout everyday life and adjusting her spending to her qualities. This model shows the groundbreaking force of moving our outlook from shortage to overflow, cultivating a feeling of satisfaction and monetary prosperity.

V. Building Strength: Exploring Monetary Difficulties

Dominating your cash mentality includes building strength to really explore monetary difficulties. Rackers recognize that monetary difficulties can happen, like employment misfortune or financial slumps. He underlines the significance of having a backup stash and keeping a drawn out point of view during testing times.

Rackers give pragmatic methodologies to building versatility, for example, expanding revenue sources, paying off past commitments, and developing an outlook of flexibility. He shares accounts of people who effectively endured monetary tempests through their flexibility and assurance. These models show the significance of planning for unexpected conditions and having a strong mentality to return from difficulties.

VI. The Convergence of Outlook and Activity: Carrying out Enduring Change

In "The Straightforward Way to Abundance," Rackers stresses that dominating your cash outlook requires activity and execution. He urges perusers to put forth clear monetary objectives, make a financial plan, and routinely keep tabs on their development. By making steady and purposeful strides, people can adjust their outlook to their monetary activities and accomplish unmistakable outcomes.

Rackers feature the groundbreaking force of responsibility and looking for help from similar people. He urges perusers to join monetary networks, go to courses, or look for direction from monetary counsels. By encircling themselves with people who share their monetary objectives, people can remain spurred and enlivened on their excursion toward monetary freedom.

Dominating your cash outlook is an excursion of self-revelation and strengthening. Through saving, effective financial planning, and living efficiently, people can reshape their relationship with cash and open the way to independence from the rat race. "The Straightforward Way to Riches

•Developing a growing long term financial stability mentality and monetary strength

Chasing monetary achievement and freedom, developing a growing long term financial stability mentality and creating monetary strength are urgent components. The manner in which we ponder cash and our mentalities toward abundance assume a huge Chapter in our monetary excursions. In this paper, we will investigate the significance of developing a strong financial foundation outlook and creating monetary strength, looking at pertinent statements and models from eminent monetary specialists and fruitful people.

I. Developing a Growing long term financial stability Outlook

A. Moving Viewpoints on Riches

Fostering a growing long term financial stability outlook requires moving points of view on riches and reclassifying our relationship with cash. As Robert Kiyosaki, creator of "Rich Father Unfortunate Father," suitably expressed, "The absolute most remarkable resource we as a whole have is our brain. Assuming that it is prepared well, it can make huge riches." This statement features the significance of outfitting the influence of our brains to make abundance.

B. Embracing Overflow and Development

To develop an establishing long term financial stability outlook, it is critical to embrace overflow and a development situated point of view. T. Harv Eker, creator of "Mysteries of the Mogul Brain," accentuates the meaning of our convictions and states, "The main explanation the vast majority don't get what they need is that they don't have any idea what they need." This statement features the significance of putting forth clear objectives and trusting in our capacity to accomplish them.

C. Conquering Restricting Convictions

Developing an establishing financial stability mentality requires testing and beating restricting convictions around cash. Suze Orman, a prestigious monetary master, urges people to have an impact on their mentality and states, "When you contemplate cash, ponder the sentiments that surface. The moment you feel those sentiments, recognize and deliver them." This statement underlines the significance of distinguishing and delivering negative convictions that might prevent our monetary advancement.

II. Creating Monetary Flexibility

A. Embracing the Force of Saving

Monetary strength includes fostering the propensity for saving. As Warren Buffett, one of the best financial backers ever, carefully expressed, "Don't save the thing that is left pursuing spending; all things being equal, spend the thing is left pursuing saving." This statement features the significance of focusing on reserve funds and building a monetary security net.

B. Going with Shrewd Venture Decisions

Creating monetary strength additionally involves pursuing savvy venture decisions. John Bogle, the pioneer behind Vanguard Gathering, underlines the worth of long haul money management and states, "The financial exchange is loaded up with people who know the cost of everything except the benefit of nothing." This statement reminds us to zero in on long haul esteem as opposed to transient market variances.

C. Exploring Monetary Difficulties

Monetary versatility includes exploring through monetary difficulties earnestly and flexibility. As Dave Ramsey, a prestigious individual budget master, expresses, "A spending plan is to let your cash know where to go as opposed to pondering where it went." This statement features the significance of having a monetary arrangement and being proactive in dealing with our funds.

III. Instances of Monetary Flexibility and Establishing a strong financial foundation Outlook

A. Oprah Winfrey

Oprah Winfrey, a news big shot, and giver, embodies the influence of establishing a strong financial foundation mentality and monetary strength. In spite of confronting huge hindrances all through her life, she embraced her energy and transformed it into a realm. Her process features the significance of trusting in oneself and daring to seek after dreams, even notwithstanding misfortune.

B. Warren Buffett

Warren Buffett's prosperity as a financial backer exhibits the influence of a growing strong financial foundation mentality and trained monetary practices. His emphasis on long haul esteem financial planning and his capacity to weather conditions market changes show the significance of persistence and an undaunted way to deal with abundance gathering.

C. Elon Musk

Elon Musk, the visionary business person behind organizations, for example, Tesla and SpaceX, embodies the crossing point of an establishing financial stability outlook and monetary versatility. In spite of various misfortunes and disappointments, Musk persisted and stayed focused on his aggressive objectives. His capacity to adjust, go ahead with carefully thought out plans of action, and think long haul has moved him to become perhaps of the most compelling figures in innovation and advancement.

End

Developing a substantial financial foundation mentality and creating monetary flexibility is fundamental for making monetary progress and freedom. By moving viewpoints on riches, embracing overflow, and defeating restricting convictions, people can open their potential to make riches. Creating monetary versatility through saving, making brilliant speculations, and exploring monetary difficulties with assurance prompts long haul monetary steadiness.

Through the instances of effective people like Oprah Winfrey, Warren Buffett, and Elon Musk, we see the influence of an establishing long term financial stability mentality and monetary versatility in real life. Their processes feature the significance of constancy, flexibility, and a drawn out center.

In outline, developing and establishing a strong financial foundation mentality and creating monetary strength requires cognizant exertion, assurance, and a readiness to challenge our convictions and ways of behaving. By embracing these standards and applying them reliably, we can change our monetary lives, accomplish our objectives, and achieve the independence from the rat race and security we want. As Tony Robbins once said, "The key to abundance is straightforward: Figure out how to accomplish more for others than any other person does. Turn out to be more significant. Accomplish more. Give more. Be more. Serve more." It is within our scope to develop a mentality that enables us to create financial stability, set out open doors, and have a constructive outcome on our daily routines and the existence of others.

CHAPTER 3

Creating Blocks of Financial wellbeing Creation

Creating financial stability is an excursion that requires strong groundwork and a reasonable guide. In "The Basic Way to Riches" by Robert D. Rackers, perusers are acquainted with the fundamental structure impedes that make ready for abundance creation and monetary autonomy. This article investigates the critical subjects and thoughts from the book, giving experiences and reasonable procedures to people looking to create their financial momentum admirably and economically.

Planning and Following Costs: The Mainstays of Monetary Achievement

At the center of abundance creation lies the essential act of planning and following costs. Rackers stresses the significance of understanding where our cash proceeds to make a spending plan that lines up with our monetary objectives. By following costs industriously and settling on informed spending choices, people can upgrade their monetary assets, focus on reserve funds and ventures, and create financial momentum over the long run.

"The Basic Way to Riches" urges perusers to embrace a parsimonious mentality, recognizing needs and needs. By testing pointless costs and diverting assets towards long-haul objectives, people can make a strong monetary establishment. Rackers advises us that embracing moderation doesn't like hardship, yet rather a careful and deliberate way to deal with spending that spotlights what genuinely gives worth and joy.

Expanding Pay: Opening the Potential for Monetary Development

While overseeing costs is significant, Rackers stresses that rising pay assumes an essential Chapter in abundance creation. The book gives bits of knowledge into systems to support procuring potential, like seeking after advanced education, getting new abilities, beginning a side business, or looking for professional success and valuable open doors. By proactively looking for ways of expanding pay, people can make a bigger monetary base from which to create their financial momentum.

Straightforwardness and Moderation: Smoothing out Monetary Lives

Chasing abundance creation, Rackers urges perusers to embrace effortlessness and moderation. By eliminating the monetary mess and intricacies, people can smooth out their monetary lives, diminishing pressure and expanding the center around long-haul objectives. Rackers features the advantages of improving on speculation methodologies, disposing of superfluous monetary items, and taking on a moderate way to deal with overseeing riches.

Contributing Shrewdly: Saddling the Force of List Assets

"The Basic Way to Riches" commits critical consideration regarding the subject of money management and features the influence of file assets as a foundation of abundance creation. Rackers demystify the intricacies of effective money management and backers for the straightforwardness and adequacy of record reserves. By putting resources into minimal expense, and latently overseeing reserves that track market records, people can profit from wide expansion, long-haul development, and negligible charges.

Rackers stresses the upsides of file support over effectively overseen reserves, which frequently accompany higher charges and neglect to outflank the market reliably. By adjusting their speculation procedure to the standards of file reserve effective money management, people can accomplish consistent and practical development while limiting dangers related to attempting to "beat the market."

Broadening and Hazard The executives: Shielding Abundance as long as possible

Broadening and chance administration are key chapters of creating and safeguarding financial stability. Rackers focuses on the significance of spreading speculations across different resource classes and enterprises to limit risk. By broadening their portfolios, people can diminish their openness to any single speculation or area and improve the probability of accomplishing stable long-haul returns.

"The Basic Way to Riches" likewise addresses the mental chapters of hazards the executives. Rackers recognizes the impulse to settle on profound choices during times of market unpredictability and offers systems for keeping a levelheaded mentality. He encourages perusers to continue through to the end, not capitulate to overreach and stay zeroed in on their drawn-out establishing long-term financial stability plans.

Making Arrangements for Retirement: Exploring the Way to Monetary Freedom

As people make progress toward monetary freedom, making arrangements for retirement turns into a critical Chapter of their excursion. "The Straightforward Way to Riches" guides enhancing retirement investment funds and going with informed choices regarding retirement accounts.

• Planning, expanding pay, and embracing effortlessness.

Achieving independence from the stoolie race is an objective that many hope for, however, it requires discipline, arranging, and key independent direction. In this paper, we will investigate three pivotal points of support on the way to monetary autonomy: planning, expanding pay, and embracing straightforwardness. By carrying out compelling techniques to lessen costs, expand pay, and embrace a modcratc mentality, people can clear their direction to an existence of independence from the rat race.

This far-reaching guide will give explicit models and pragmatic counsel on the best way to set aside cash, contribute admirably, and take full advantage of accessible assets.

I. Planning: Assuming Command over Your Funds

Planning is the groundwork of monetary achievement. It includes cautiously checking and assigning pay to different costs, reserve funds, and ventures. By making a practical financial plan, people gain a reasonable comprehension of their monetary circumstances and can settle on informed conclusions about their ways of managing money. Here are a few methodologies to lessen costs and set aside cash:

1. Track Costs: Begin by examining your spending designs and sorting your costs. Use planning instruments or applications to follow your exchanges and recognize regions where you can scale back.

2. Focus on Needs Over Cares: Recognize fundamental requirements and optional needs. Center around covering fundamental costs like lodging, utilities, food, and medical services before apportioning assets to optional things.

3. Reduce Superfluous Expenses:
Recognize regions where you can decrease costs without undermining your satisfaction. This might incorporate dropping unused memberships, arranging lower bills, or tracking down financially savvy choices.

4. Embrace Thriftiness: Foster an economical outlook by embracing cognizant ways of managing money and keeping away from motivation buys. Consider getting or leasing as opposed to purchasing, and practice careful utilization.

II. Expanding Pay:

Augmenting Your Acquiring Potential

While overseeing costs is significant, expanding pay can altogether speed up the excursion to independence from the rat race. Here are systems to support your acquiring potential:

1. Improve Abilities and Schooling:
Put resources into procuring new abilities or seeking extra training that can prompt professional success or more lucrative open doors.

2. Begin a Side Business:
Investigate pioneering tries by sending off a side business or adapting a leisure activity or energy. This can turn out an extra revenue stream and expected long-haul development.

3. Look for Pay Discussion:
Exploration market pay rates and haggle for better remuneration while beginning a new position or during execution surveys. Appropriately well-spoken about your worth to the association and be positive about supporting fair remuneration.

4. Numerous Revenue Sources:
Expand your pay sources by investigating independent work, temporary positions, or recurring sources of income like investment properties or speculations.

III. Embracing Straightforwardness: The Force of Moderation

Straightforwardness is a crucial role in accomplishing independence from the rat race. Embracing a moderate way of life permits people to decrease the monetary mess, center around the main thing, and distribute assets proficiently. Here are systems to embrace straightforwardness and enhance your monetary assets:

1. Clean up and Sell Undesirable Things: Clean up your living spaces and sell unused or superfluous things. Besides the fact that this makes actual space, it likewise creates extra pay.

2. Focus on Encounters Over Material Belongings: Shift your concentration from

amassing material belongings to putting resources into encounters and significant connections. Assign assets to exercises that give enduring joy and individual satisfaction.

3. Smooth out Ventures: Work on your speculation portfolio by combining records and zeroing in on the minimal expense, and expanded list reserves. Keep away from pointless intricacy and charges related to effectively oversaw reserves.

4. Computerize Reserve funds and Ventures: Set up programmed moves from your check to reserve funds and speculation accounts. This guarantees steady commitments without depending on self-control alone.

5. 5. Practice Careful Spending: Before making buys, inquire as to whether the thing lines up with your qualities and on the off chance that it brings long haul esteem. It's critical to take advantage of your assets by saving and contributing shrewdly. Here are a few key systems:

1. Secret stash: Fabricate a secret stash to cover surprising costs and give a well-being net. Go for the gold and a half year of everyday costs in a promptly open bank account.

2. Obligation The executives: Focus on taking care of exorbitant interest obligations, for example, Mastercard obligations or individual advances. Foster a reimbursement plan that lines up with your spending plan and consider merging obligations to bring down loan fees if possible.

3. Retirement Reserve funds: Contribute consistently to retirement accounts, for example, manager-supported 401(k) plans or individual retirement accounts (IRAs). Exploit any business matching commitments and consider augmenting your commitments to profit from charge benefits and long-haul development potential.

4. Long haul Speculations: Designate a piece of your investment funds to long haul ventures, for

example, minimal expense file reserves or broadened arrangement of stocks and securities. Contribute reliably over the long run to profit from intensifying returns and moderate momentary market variances.

5. Standard Audit and Change: Consistently survey what is going on and change your spending plan, reserve funds, and growth strategies depending on the situation. Remain informed about monetary business sectors and look for proficient counsel when vital.

End

Creating financial momentum and accomplishing independence from the rat race requires a mix of trained planning, expanding pay, and embracing effortlessness. By lessening costs, boosting pay, and embracing a moderate mentality, people can dispense assets all the more proficiently and make progress toward their monetary objectives. Moreover, saving and contributing shrewdly permit people to capitalize on their assets and fabricate a strong starting point for long-haul monetary security.

"The Basic Way to Riches" offers important bits of knowledge and methodologies to help people on their excursion to independence from the rat race. By carrying out the structure blocks of planning, expanding pay, and embracing effortlessness, people can clear their direction to an existence of monetary freedom, security, and true serenity. It's essential that creating financial well-being is a continuous interaction, and it requires persistence, diligence, and a guarantee of long-haul monetary objectives. With an unmistakable arrangement and assurance, anybody can leave on the way to independence from the rat race and make a more promising time to come for themselves as well as their friends and family.

CHAPTER 4

Contributing 101: A Novice's Aide

Contributing is a useful asset that permits people to develop their riches and accomplish monetary objectives. Notwithstanding, for novices, exploring the universe of ventures can be dismaying. In this complete aid, we will dig into the fundamentals of effective money management, giving fundamental information and methodologies to assist novices with getting everything rolling on their speculation process. From understanding various kinds of speculations and their related dangers to building a very broadened portfolio, this guide intends to engage people with the information they need to settle on informed venture choices and expand their drawn-out returns.

I. Grasping Speculation Nuts and bolts

1. Characterizing Ventures:
We start by characterizing what speculation is and why it is a significant Chapter of creating financial momentum. We investigate the idea of giving cash something to do to produce returns after some time.

2. Various Kinds of Speculations:
We talk about different venture choices, including stocks, securities, shared reserves, trade exchange reserves (ETFs), land, and elective ventures. Each type has its qualities, advantages, and dangers, furnishing people with an expansive scope of decisions to suit their speculation inclinations and hazard resilience.

3. Surveying Hazard:
Understanding and overseeing risk is fundamental for effective contributing. We dive into the idea of hazard and return compromise, investigating how chance levels fluctuate across various sorts of speculations and methodologies for moderating gamble.

II. Fostering a Speculation Technique

1. Putting forth Monetary Objectives:
Before leaving on a speculation venture, characterizing your monetary goals is essential. We guide users on the most proficient method to set reasonable present moment and long haul objectives, considering variables like time skyline, pay, and change resilience.

2. Resource Allotment:
Resource designation alludes to the dissemination of speculations across various resource classes, like stocks, bonds, and money. We examine the significance of resource designation and guide on deciding the ideal allotment given individual objectives and change resistance.

3. Expansion:
Enhancement is a vital methodology for overseeing risk. We make sense of the idea of broadening and its advantages, underscoring the significance of spreading ventures across various

areas, geographic districts, and resource classes. Contextual investigations and models show the way that broadening can assist with limiting misfortunes and upgrading general portfolio execution.

4. Minimizing risk:
Mitigating risk is an efficient speculation system that includes financial planning and a decent measure of cash at ordinary spans. We make sense of how this procedure can assist with moderating the effect of market unpredictability and possibly upgrade returns over the long haul.

III. Getting everything rolling with Ventures

1. Speculation Records:
We investigate various sorts of venture accounts, including individual money market funds, retirement accounts (e.g., 401(k) and IRAs), and schooling investment accounts (e.g., 529 plans). Perusers gain a comprehension of the assessment benefits, commitment cutoff points, and withdrawal rules related to each kind of record.

2. Picking a Venture Stage:

We give an outline of famous speculation stages and representatives, featuring key elements, expenses, and easy-to-use interfaces. This data engages novices to choose a stage that lines up with their speculation needs and inclinations.

3. Investigating and Choosing Ventures:

We guide perusers on the most proficient method to lead examination and investigation to go with informed speculation choices. This incorporates assessing organization basics, breaking down market drifts, and taking into account factors like valuation, development potential, and industry viewpoint.

4. Long haul Money management:

We underline the advantages of a drawn-out speculation approach. Through authentic information and contextual analyses, we show how intensifying returns and remaining contributed overstretched periods can prompt huge abundance amassing.

IV. Risk The executives and Checking

1. Ordinary Portfolio Audit:
We stress the significance of checking and investigating venture portfolios routinely. We give rules on evaluating portfolio execution, rebalancing, and making essential acclimations to line up with changing objectives and economic situations.

2. Risk The executive's Methodologies:
We talk about risk-the-board strategies to safeguard speculations and limit likely misfortunes. This incorporates setting stop-misfortune orders, expanding across resource classes, and taking into account speculation choices with lower instability.

3. Grasping Business sector Unpredictability:
We address the certainty of market vacillations and the significance of remaining restrained during times of instability. We give techniques to deal with feelings and try not to pursue rash speculation choices given transient market developments.

4. Significance of Speculation Schooling:
We stress the requirement for continuous venture instruction and remain informed about market patterns, financial pointers, and industry improvements. We suggest dependable wellsprings of data and assets to extend information and settle on very much educated speculation choices.

V. Checking and Changing Speculation Techniques

1. Rebalancing:
Rebalancing includes intermittently changing the portfolio's resource assignment to keep up with the ideal gamble and bring the profile back. We guide when and how to rebalance ventures to guarantee arrangements with monetary objectives and hazard resilience.

2. Charge Contemplations:
We investigate the expense ramifications of different venture choices, including capital addition assessments, profits, and

duty-proficient speculation techniques. Understanding the assessment of effective money management can assist people with improving after-government forms and limiting charge liabilities.

3. Looking for Proficient Exhortation:
While independent financial planning is available and engaging, we recognize the benefit of looking for proficient guidance when required. We examine situations where people might profit from the skill of monetary consultants and give tips for tracking down trustworthy experts.

End
Contributing 101:
A Fledgling's Aide outfits people with the essential information and techniques expected to set out on an effective speculation venture. By grasping various sorts of ventures, overseeing risk through enhancement, and fostering a trained speculation approach, perusers can lay the foundation for long-haul abundance creation. The aide underscores the significance of laying out monetary objectives, remaining

informed, and ceaselessly checking and changing venture systems to line up with evolving conditions. By following the standards illustrated in this aid, fledglings can acquire trust in their venture choices, expand returns, and fabricate a strong starting point for their monetary future. Keep in mind, contributing is an excursion that requires tolerance, discipline, and a drawn-out viewpoint. With the right information and outlook, anybody can turn into a fruitful financial backer and accomplish their monetary objectives.

• Outline of venture vehicles, stocks, securities, and common assets.

Contributing is an amazing asset for creating financial stability and accomplishing monetary objectives. To set out on a fruitful speculation venture, it is significant to comprehend the various kinds of speculation vehicles accessible. In this extensive outline, we will investigate three principal speculation vehicles: stocks, securities, and common assets. We will talk about their qualities, dangers, and advantages, and make sense of how they can be utilized to bul. Qualities: Securities are obligation protections given by states, regions, or enterprises to raise capital. Financial backers loan cash to the guarantor in return for ordinary premium installments (coupon) and the arrival of the head at development.

2. Chances:
Security ventures convey different dangers, including loan fee risk, credit hazard, and expansion risk. Changes in loan costs can influence bond costs, and credit risk mirrors the guarantor's capacity to reimburse the obligation. Expansion disintegrates the buying force of fixed coupon installments.

3. Benefits:
Bonds turn out stable revenue through standard coupon installments, making them appropriate for money-centered financial backers. They likewise offer capital conservation and can act as a support against value market instability.

4. Model:

A financial backer approaching retirement and looking to produce reliable pay might dispense a huge Chapter of their portfolio to excellent corporate securities or government securities, going for the gold installments and capital protection.

III. Shared Assets: Expertly Oversaw Portfolios

1. Qualities:

Shared reserves pool cash from numerous financial backers to put resources into a differentiated arrangement of stocks, bonds, or different resources. They are expertly overseen by reserve administrators, who go with venture choices for the benefit of the financial backers.

2. Gambles:

Common subsidies convey chances related to the fundamental resources they hold. Furthermore, charges and costs related to common assets can affect generally speaking returns.

3. Benefits:

Common finances offer enhancement across a scope of resources, giving admittance to expertly oversaw portfolios in any event, for individual financial backers with restricted capital. They offer accommodation, liquidity, and the chance to put resources into Chapter ocular areas or markets.

4. Model:

A financial backer searching for expansive market openness and enhancement might put resources into a record store, which plans to imitate the exhibition of a Chapter ocular market list. For example, a financial backer looking for openness to the S&P 500 file might put resources into an S&P 500 record shared reserve.

IV. Building a Differentiated Portfolio

1. Enhancement Advantages: Broadening is a methodology that includes spreading ventures across various resource classes and protections to diminish risk. By putting resources into a

blend of stocks, securities, and common assets, financial backers can bring down the effect of any singular venture's exhibition on their general portfolio.

2. Resource Designation: Resource allotment alludes to the dissemination of ventures across various resource classes. Financial backers can tailor their resource designation given their gamble resistance, speculation objectives, and time skyline. A very broad portfolio ordinarily incorporates a mix of stocks, securities, and common assets.

3. Rebalancing: Standard portfolio rebalancing guarantees that the resource assignment stays by the financial backer's ideal gamble profile. By intermittently inspecting and changing the portfolio, financial backers can keep up with their ideal gamble return equilibrium and catch open doors for development.

Model: A financial backer with a moderate gamble resilience and a drawn-out speculation skyline might designate 60% of their portfolio to a blend of stocks and common assets for development potential while dispensing 40% to securities for soundness and pay age. This assignment adjusts the longing for development with risk alleviation.

V. Contemplations for Venture Vehicles

Time Skyline: The venture vehicle picked ought to line up with the financial backer's time skyline. Longer-term objectives might warrant a higher distribution to development-situated speculations like stocks, while more limited-term objectives might require a more prominent accentuation on security and pay from bonds.

Risk Resistance: Financial backers ought to survey their gamble resilience to decide the fitting designation for various venture vehicles. Those OK with higher gambling might have a higher distribution to stocks, while more gamble loath people might settle on a bigger bond designation.

Expansion: Differentiating across speculation vehicles diminishes the effect of any single venture's exhibition. It spreads risk across various resource classes, areas, and districts, improving the potential for stable returns over the long haul.

Research and A reasonable level of effort: Financial backers ought to lead exhaustive exploration and an expected level of effort before putting resources into a specific speculation vehicle. This incorporates evaluating verifiable execution, investigating charges and costs, and grasping the venture's essentials.

VI. High-level Venture Systems

1. Area Explicit Money management: A few financial backers might decide to zero in on unambiguous areas or businesses that they accept will outflank the more extensive market. This technique expects top-to-bottom examination and comprehension of the picked area's elements and patterns.

2. Esteem Effective money management: Worth financial backers look for stocks that are underestimated by the market, with the conviction that their actual characteristic worth will be perceived after some time. This approach includes distinguishing stocks exchanged at a rebate compared with their essentials.

3. Development Contributing: Development financial backers center around organizations with solid development potential, frequently ready to pay a premium for stocks expected to convey better-than-expected income development. This procedure requires recognizing organizations in businesses with high development possibilities.

4. Profit Effective financial planning: Profit-centered financial backers focus on stocks or shared reserves that turn out standard revenue through profit installments. This approach is appropriate for money looking for financial backers, especially those in or approaching retirement.

5. Minimizing risk: Mitigating risk implies financial planning and a decent measure of cash at standard stretches, no matter what the venture's cost. This methodology permits financial backers to purchase more offers when costs are low and fewer offers when costs are high, possibly decreasing the effect of momentary market unpredictability.

6. Record Asset Contributing: File reserves are shared assets or trade exchanged reserves (ETFs) intended to imitate the exhibition of a Chapter ocular market list, like the S&P 500. This detached speculation procedure plans to match the market's general exhibition instead of beating it.

VII. Observing and Changing the Portfolio

1. Customary Portfolio Audit: Financial backers ought to consistently survey their portfolios to guarantee they stay lined up with their objectives and hazard resilience. This includes evaluating individual speculations' exhibitions, investigating

the general resource portion, and making important changes.

2. Rebalancing: As economic situations and individual ventures' presentation change, it is vital to balance the portfolio to keep up with the ideal resource designation. This cycle includes selling or purchasing resources to align the portfolio back with the objective distribution.

3. Charge Contemplations: Financial backers ought to know about the duty ramifications of their venture choices. Techniques, for example, charge misfortune gathering, holding interests in charge of advantaged records, and understanding the expense treatment of profits and capital additions can assist with streamlining after-expense forms.

4. Nonstop Learning and Schooling: The speculation scene is dynamic, and remaining informed is critical. Financial backers ought to consistently look for information, remain refreshed on market drifts, and adjust their techniques depending on the situation.

Putting resources into various kinds of speculation vehicles offers people a scope of chances to develop their riches, create pay, and accomplish their monetary objectives. Stocks give proprietorship in organizations and the potential for capital appreciation, securities offer solidness and pay, while common assets give proficient administration and enhancement. By grasping the qualities, dangers, and advantages of every speculation vehicle, financial backers can develop very much broadened portfolios custom fitted to their time skyline, risk resistance, and objectives. High-level methodologies, for example, are explicit money management, esteem financial planning, and development contributing can be used for additional designated approaches. Ordinary portfolio surveys, rebalancing, and charge contemplations are fundamental for keeping a very much upgraded portfolio. Persistent learning and remaining informed are essential in exploring the always-advancing venture scene. With a cautious examination, vital preparation, and restrained execution, people can pursue informed venture choices and work toward their monetary desires. Keep in mind, contributing implies dangers, and looking for proficient counsel or direction is suggested for *customized* venture systems.

CHAPTER 5

Planning Your Money growth strategy;

A Nitty gritty Arrangement

1. Characterize Your Monetary Objectives
- Begin by recognizing your monetary objectives, both the present moment and the long haul. Models might incorporate putting something aside for retirement, buying a home, subsidizing schooling, or beginning a business.
- - Measure every objective by connecting a Chapter ocular dollar sum and an objective timetable for accomplishing it.
-
- 2. Survey Your Gamble Resistance
- - Assess your gambling resilience by thinking about your monetary

circumstance, speculation information, and solace level with market changes.

- - Comprehend that higher-risk speculations have the potential for more noteworthy returns, yet, in addition, accompany expanded unpredictability and likely misfortunes.

-

- 3. Decide Your Venture Methodology
- - Settle the kind of speculations that line up with your objectives and change resistance. Consider a blend of various speculation vehicles like stocks, securities, common assets, land, and elective ventures.
- - Think about the likely returns, dangers, and liquidity of every venture type.

-

- 4. Set Resource Portion
- - Decide the proper resource assignment in light of your objectives, risk resilience, and time skyline. Resource designation alludes to the level of your portfolio dispensed to various resource classes.

- - Balance your portfolio by broadening across resource classes to diminish risk. Think about variables like your age, venture objectives, and economic situations while deciding your resource distribution.
-
- 5. Research and Select Speculations
-
- - Lead careful examination of likely ventures. Think about elements like verifiable execution, the monetary well-being of the organization or asset, the executive's mastery, charges, and costs.
- - Differentiate your ventures inside every resource class to additionally alleviate risk. Pick a blend of development-situated speculations and pay-producing resources.
-
- 6. Execute a Customary Growth strategy
- - Set up a standard growth strategy, for example, robotized commitments to your speculation accounts. Steady

commitments help to exploit mitigating risk and lessen the effect of market instability.

- - Rebalance your portfolio occasionally to keep up with your ideal resource allotment. This includes selling overperforming resources and purchasing failing to meet expectations resources to realign with your objective portion.

-

- 7. Screen and Survey Your Portfolio
- - Consistently survey the presentation of your speculations and evaluate their arrangement with your objectives. Remain informed about market patterns and financial variables that might affect your speculations.
- - Make acclimations to your portfolio depending on the situation given changes in your monetary circumstance, risk resilience, or economic situations.

-

- 8. Look for Proficient Counsel
- - Consider talking with a monetary counsel who can give customized

direction and assist with upgrading your venture procedure.

- - A consultant can help with fostering a complete monetary arrangement, give venture proposals, and give continuous portfolios to the board.

-

- 9. Oversee Dangers
- - Know about the dangers related to various ventures. Comprehend that better yields frequently accompany higher gambling.
- - Differentiate your portfolio across different resource classes and ventures to spread risk.
- - Consistently evaluate and deal with the dangers inside your portfolio, changing your system depending on the situation.

-

- 10. Remain Educated and Taught

-

- - Constantly instruct yourself about money management and monetary business sectors. Remain refreshed on speculation news, financial patterns, and changes in guidelines that might affect your ventures.

- - Consistently audit your money growth strategy, looking for valuable chances to improve and upgrade your portfolio procedure.

-

- Keep in mind, planning a speculation portfolio is a customized cycle. Consider working with a monetary consultant to fit your arrangement of your chapter's ocular monetary objectives, risk resistance, and time skyline. Routinely screen and survey your portfolio to remain focused and make changes on a case-by-case basis. Know about the dangers implied in effective money management and be ready to likewise adjust your procedure.

•Defining objectives and overseeing speculation chances.

Defining clear objectives and overseeing venture chances are essential components in making long-haul monetary progress. Without an unmistakable vision of what you need to achieve and a proactive way to deal with overseeing gambles, your venture process can become unfocused and possibly negative to your monetary prosperity. In this exposition, we will investigate the meaning of defining clear objectives, examine procedures for accomplishing those objectives, and feature the potential dangers related to financial planning.

Defining clear objectives gives guidance and motivation to your venture methodology. By characterizing your monetary targets, whether it's putting something aside for retirement, buying a home, or subsidizing your kids' schooling, you can adjust your speculation choices to these objectives. Clear objectives help you focus on and settle on informed decisions about where to distribute your assets. They likewise give inspiration and a feeling of progress as you pursue accomplishing every achievement. To oversee venture chances, enhancement is a key system. Enhancing your venture portfolio across various resource classes, businesses, and geological locales helps spread risk and decrease the effect of any single speculation's presentation. By having a blend of stocks, securities, land, and other speculation vehicles, you can relieve the potential misfortunes that might emerge from market variances. Also, occasional portfolio rebalancing guarantees that your speculations stay lined up with your gamble resistance and objectives.

One more system for overseeing venture gambles is leading careful examination and an expected level of effort before settling on speculation choices. Understanding the basics of every venture, for example, the organization's monetary well-being, industry patterns, and the board's ability, permits you to settle on additional educated decisions. Also, remaining informed about market patterns, monetary pointers, and administrative changes empowers you to in like manner adjust your speculation methodology.

While financial planning offers the potential for monetary development, it is vital to recognize and deal with the dangers related to it. Market instability, financial slumps, and unanticipated occasions can affect the worth of ventures. It is urgent to keep a drawn-out point of view and not respond imprudently to momentary market variances. Moreover, keeping a secret stash can give a well-being net during unforeseen monetary difficulties, diminishing the need to sell speculations at troublesome times.

Financial backers ought to likewise know about conduct inclinations that can cloud judgment and lead to unfortunate navigation. Profound responses to showcase swings, for example, alarm selling during a slump or pursuing patterns during market tops, can be negative to long-haul monetary achievement. Fostering a trained and sane way to deal with effective financial planning, given distinct objectives and a sound speculation system, beats these predispositions.

In any case, it means quite a bit to take note that no venture procedure is without chances. Potential dangers include the chance of a deficiency of head, expansion dissolving the buying force of your ventures, and the vulnerability related to explicit enterprises or districts. It is fundamental to survey your gamble resistance and know about the dangers implied in various venture choices. Looking for proficient counsel from monetary consultants or abundance chiefs can give important bits of knowledge and assist with relieving gambles.

All in all, laying out clear objectives and overseeing venture chances are basic Chapters for making long-haul monetary progress. Clear objectives give guidance and inspiration while overseeing takes a chance through broadening, rescarching, and kccping a traincd way to deal with protecting your speculations. Monitoring expected dangers and understanding your gamble resilience considers informed independent direction. By integrating these procedures into your venture process, you can explore the always-changing monetary scene and work towards getting your drawn-out monetary prosperity.

CHAPTER 6

List Assets: The Force of Straightforwardness

Opening the Force of File Assets: Embracing Straightforwardness for Venture Achievement

In the high-speed universe of effective money management, where complex procedures and refined venture vehicles overwhelm the titles, there exists a basic yet incredible asset that has unobtrusively changed the scene of abundance gathering: file reserves. These honest speculation vehicles have acquired far-reaching ubiquity lately and for good explanation. With their direct methodology and history of conveying strong returns, file subsidies offer a convincing venture procedure that can help financial backers of all degrees of skill.

All in all, what precisely are file assets and for what reason would they say they are such an extraordinary decision for financial backers? At their center, file reserves are a sort of common asset or trade exchange store (ETF) that intends to recreate the exhibition of a Chapter ocular market list, like the S&P 500 or the FTSE 100. Rather than depending on dynamic administration and endeavoring to outflank the market, list reserves inactively track the exhibition of the basic record by holding an expanded arrangement of protections that reflect the file's piece. This latent methodology works on the venture interaction as well as assisting with minimizing expenses, as record reserves commonly have lower cost proportions contrasted with effectively oversaw reserves.

One of the vital benefits of file subsidies lies in their capacity to give wide market openness and moment expansion. By putting resources into a list store, you get sufficiently close to a container of stocks or securities that address a specific market section. This expansion assists with spreading risk and decreases the effect of individual stock or area instability on your general portfolio. Dissimilar to individual stock picking, which expects top-to-bottom exploration and the capacity to precisely anticipate market patterns, list reserves permit financial backers to Chapter to take in the development of the general market without the requirement for consistent checking or making dangerous wagers on individual organizations.

Besides, the straightforwardness of record subsidies goes with them a great decision for both prepared financial backers and novices to the venture world. Indeed, even amazing financial backer Warren Buffett himself has suggested file assets for most of the financial backers, referring to their low expenses and long-haul execution as convincing motivations to embrace this venture technique. With record reserves, you needn't bother with being a monetary wizard or go through hours examining market information. The assets accomplish the work for you, reflecting the exhibition of the picked file, while you can zero in on different Chapters of your life or seek after your interests.

One more outstanding advantage of list reserves is their expense productivity. Because of their latent nature, file reserves for most Chapters have lower turnover contrasted with effectively overseen reserves. This results in fewer capital additions and appropriations, which can assist with diminishing your duty responsibility. Furthermore, the purchase-and-hold approach of record reserves adjusts well to the system of long-haul financial planning, permitting you to profit from intensifying returns and possibly bring down your general taxation rate.

It's worth focusing on that while file reserves give magnificent market openness and expansion, they are not sans risk. Market vacillations ca aspects of their exhibition, and they are dependent upon the intrinsic dangers related to the Chapter ocular modular recorded the track any case, by keeping a drawn-out venture skyline and reliably adding to your file store property, you can brave momentary unpredictability and possibly benefit from the general development of the market.

While considering file assets as a feature of your venture methodology, it is crucial for a direct intensive examination and selecting assets that line up with your speculation objectives and change resilience. Search for legitimate asset suppliers with a history of low expenses, effective following of the picked file, and solid client support. Furthermore, consider the Chapter ocular file being followed, as various lists center around different market areas or locales.

To make the most of your index fund investment, consider the following tips:

1. Determine your investment goals: Before investing in index funds, define your financial objectives. Are you saving for retirement, a down payment on a house, or your child's education? Establishing clear goals will help you choose the appropriate index funds that align with your objectives.

2. Understand the index being trackcd: Different index funds track various market indexes. Some focus on broad market indices like the S&P 500,

while others may target specific sectors or regions. Understand the composition and performance history of the index to ensure it matches your investment strategy and risk tolerance.

3. Diversify across asset classes: While index funds inherently offer diversification within the asset class they track, it's also important to diversify across different asset classes. Consider adding bond index funds or international equity index funds to your portfolio to further spread risk and capture opportunities in different market segments.

4. Keep costs low: One of the significant advantages of index funds is their lower expense ratios compared to actively managed funds. Look for funds with minimal fees and expenses to maximize your investment returns. Remember, even a small difference in expense ratios can have a significant impact on your long-term wealth accumulation.

5. Stay the course: Index funds are designed for long-term investing. Avoid making impulsive decisions based on short-term market fluctuations. Stick to your investment plan and avoid trying to time the market. Consistent contributions and a disciplined approach will yield better results over time.

6. Rebalance periodically: As market conditions change, your portfolio may deviate from your intended asset allocation. Periodic rebalancing ensures that your portfolio remains in line with your risk tolerance and investment goals. Rebalancing involves selling over performing assets and reinvesting in underperforming assets to maintain the desired allocation.

7. Seek professional advice if needed: If you are unsure about which index funds to choose or need guidance in constructing your investment portfolio, consider seeking advice from a financial advisor or investment professional. They can provide personalized recommendations based on your specific financial situation and goals.

In conclusion, index funds offer a powerful investment strategy that embraces simplicity, diversification, and low costs. By investing in these funds, you gain broad market exposure, instant diversification, and the potential for long-term wealth accumulation. However, as with any investment, it is crucial to do your due diligence, set clear goals, and stay disciplined in your approach. With the right strategy and a long-term mindset, index funds can be a powerful tool in achieving your financial goals and securing your financial future.

• Benefits of file reserves and choosing them for development.

Index funds have emerged as a popular investment vehicle, offering numerous advantages for investors seeking long-term growth and a passive approach to wealth accumulation. In this article, we will explore the advantages of investing in index funds and discuss the considerations that should be taken into account when selecting these funds.

Advantages of Index Funds for Growth:

1. Broad Market Exposure: Index funds provide investors with exposure to a broad market index, such as the S&P 500 or the NASDAQ. By investing in an index fund, you gain ownership in a diversified portfolio of stocks or bonds that represent a specific market segment. This broad exposure allows you to Chapter anticipate the overall growth of the market, capturing the performance of multiple companies or sectors.

2. Instant Diversification: Diversification is a key component of a successful investment strategy. Index funds inherently offer instant diversification by holding a basket of securities that mirror the composition of the index they track. This diversification helps spread risk across different companies, industries, and regions, reducing the impact of any single investment's performance on your overall portfolio.

3. Cost Efficiency: Index funds are known for their cost efficiency. Compared to actively managed funds, which rely on extensive research and incur higher management fees, index funds follow a passive investment approach. They aim to replicate the performance of an index rather than outperform it. As a result, index funds tend to have lower expense ratios, saving investors money over the long term.

4. Consistent Performance: While index funds do not guarantee superior returns, historical data has shown that many index funds have delivered competitive and consistent performance over time. By capturing the overall market performance, index funds have the potential to generate satisfactory returns that align with the performance of the index they track.

Considerations When Selecting Index Funds:

1. Objective and Strategy: Before investing in index funds, clarify your investment objective and risk tolerance. Different index funds track

various market indices, including broad market indices, sector-specific indices, and international indices. Understand the objective and strategy of the index fund you are considering to ensure it aligns with your investment goals.

2. Tracking Error: While index funds aim to replicate the performance of an index, some funds may have a tracking error. This discrepancy occurs due to factors such as fees, expenses, and imperfect replication of the index's composition. Compare the tracking error of different funds to choose the one that closely matches the index's performance.

3. Expense Ratio: The expense ratio represents the annual operating expenses of an index fund as a percentage of its total assets. Lower expense ratios are generally preferable, as they reduce the drag on investment returns. Compare expense ratios among similar index funds to find the most cost-effective option.

4. Liquidity: Consider the liquidity of the index fund you are interested in. Higher liquidity

ensures that you can easily buy or sell shares without significantly impacting the market price. Ensure that the index fund has sufficient trading volume and a narrow bid-ask spread for ease of transactions.

5. Index Construction Methodology: Different index funds may use different methodologies to construct their portfolios. Understand the index construction methodology employed by the fund, such as market capitalization-weighted, equal-weighted, or fundamentally weighted. Each methodology has its characteristics and may result in variations in performance.

6. Rebalancing Frequency: Some index funds may have a predetermined rebalancing frequency, where the fund periodically adjusts its holdings to maintain the desired index composition. Consider the rebalancing frequency and its potential impact on transaction costs and tax implications.

7. Risk Considerations: While index funds offer diversification, they are still subject to market

risks. The performance of an index fund will closely track the performance of the underlying index. Understand the potential risks associated with the specific market index being tracked, such as market volatility, economic factors, and geopolitical events. It's important to evaluate the risks associated with the underlying assets in the index, such as industry-specific risks or credit risks in bond index funds.

8. Tax Efficiency: Index funds generally have a lower turnover rate compared to actively managed funds. This lower turnover can result in fewer capital gains distributions, leading to potential tax advantages for investors. Consider the tax efficiency of the index fund, especially if you are investing in a taxable account.

9. Investor Education: Before investing in index funds, educate yourself about the fundamentals of investing, including concepts like asset allocation, risk management, and portfolio rebalancing. Understanding these principles will help you make informed decisions and stay

committed to your investment strategy over the long term.

10. Long-Term Perspective: Index funds are ideally suited for long-term investors. While short-term market fluctuations can be unsettling, it's important to maintain a long-term perspective and resist the temptation to make impulsive investment decisions based on short-term market movements. Stay focused on your investment goals and be patient.

In conclusion, investing in index funds offers numerous advantages for investors seeking growth in their portfolios. With their broad market exposure, instant diversification, cost efficiency, and potential for consistent performance, index funds provide a simple and effective way to Chapter anticipate the overall growth of the market. When selecting index funds, consider factors such as the fund's objective, tracking error, expense ratio, liquidity, index construction methodology, and risk considerations. It's important to have a clear investment objective, a long-term perspective, and a commitment to regularly review and rebalance your portfolio. By harnessing the power of index funds and adhering to a disciplined investment approach, investors can position themselves for long-term financial success. As always, it's advisable to consult with a financial advisor or investment professional to ensure that index funds align with your individual financial goals and risk tolerance.

CHAPTER 7

Exploring Retirement Arranging

Retirement is a huge life achievement that denotes another Chapter loaded up with valuable open doors and difficulties. As you leave on your retirement arranging venture, it's significant to think about the monetary viewpoints, expect the way of life changes, and plan for potential difficulties that might emerge during this progress. In this article, we will investigate these three critical regions to assist you with exploring your retirement arranging actually.

Monetary Contemplations:

1. Evaluating Retirement Pay: Decide your normal kinds of revenue in retirement, for example, annuity plans, Government managed retirement advantages and individual reserve funds. Assess whether your projected pay will be adequate to cover your ideal way of life and costs during retirement.

2. Making a Retirement Financial Plan: Foster an exhaustive financial plan that mirrors your expected costs in retirement. Consider factors, for example, lodging, medical services costs, travel, side interests, and potential long-haul care needs. A very arranged financial plan will give a structure to dealing with your funds and guaranteeing that your retirement investment funds last all through your retirement years.

3. Augmenting Retirement Reserve funds: Exploit retirement reserve funds vehicles like 401(k) plans, individual retirement accounts (IRAs), and other speculation choices. Audit your venture procedure, resource allotment, and hazard resistance to upgrade your portfolio for likely development and pay age.

4. Overseeing Medical Services Expenses: Medical care costs can fundamentally influence your retirement funds. Grasp Federal medical care qualification, inclusion choiccs, and supplemental protection intends to guarantee satisfactory medical care during retirement.

Consider the likely requirement for long-haul care protection to safeguard against future clinical and care costs.

Way of life Changes:

1. Rethinking Your Personality: Retirement frequently includes a change in character, as you progress from a vocation-centered person to somebody embracing another way of life. Carve out the opportunity to ponder your inclinations, interests, and objectives in retirement. Investigate new side interests, volunteer, open doors, or do seasonal work to keep a feeling of direction and satisfaction.

2. Social Associations: Building and sustaining social associations is vital during retirement. Search out friendly exercises, local gatherings, or clubs that line up with your inclinations. Remain associated with companions, family, and Chapter news to keep areas of strength for an organization and battle sensations of seclusion.

3. Changing Living Courses of Action: Consider whether your ongoing everyday environment is reasonable for retirement. Assess factors like lodging costs, openness, vicinity to medical care offices, and the longing for a dynamic local area. You might decide to scale back, move, or investigate other lodging choices that line up with your retirement way of life and monetary objectives.

4. Using time effectively: Retirement offers an overflow of available energy, and overseeing it is fundamental. Make a normal that incorporates actual work, mental feeling, and relaxation exercises. Thinking about chasing after long-lasting learning, travel, or taking Chapter is in a humanitarian effort to keep a satisfying and dynamic retirement way of life.

Possible Difficulties:

1. Life span and Monetary Maintainability: Expanding the future means anticipating a more extended retirement period. Guarantee that your retirement reserve funds and speculation

procedure are lined up with your normal life expectancy to keep away from the gamble of outlasting your assets.

2. Market Unpredictability: Variances in the monetary business sectors can affect your retirement reserve funds. Lay out an enhanced speculation portfolio that adjusts hazard and return. Occasionally audit and change your ventures to adjust to changing economic situations.

3. Medical services Expenses and Long haul Care: Rising medical care costs, including long haul care costs, can represent a test during retirement. Research and consider protection choices to moderate expected monetary weights. Integrate medical care costs into your retirement planning and investigate systems to safeguard against surprising clinical costs.

4. Expansion and Cost for most everyday items: After some time, the expense of labor and products will in general rise because of expansion. Represent expansion in your

retirement wanting to keep up with your buying power. Consider speculations that give expansion changed revenue sources, for example, Depository Expansion Safeguarded Protections (TIPS).

*NavigatingRetirement Arranging: Looking for Proficient Direction and Backing:

1. Counsel a Monetary Consultant: Looking for direction from a certified monetary guide who can assist you with exploring the intricacies of retirement arranging. A counsel can evaluate what is happening, give customized methodologies, and assist you with settling on informed choices to accomplish your retirement objectives.

2. Home Preparation: Foster an exhaustive bequest plan that incorporates a will, legal authority, and medical services mandates. Bequest arranging guarantees that your resources are dispersed by your desires and can assist with limiting duty liabilities. Work with a bequest arranging lawyer to guarantee your

reports are exceptional and mirror your ongoing conditions.

3. Remain Informed: Keep yourself informed about changes in charge regulations, retirement approaches, and venture patterns. Keeping awake to date with monetary news and going to instructive courses or studios can upgrade your monetary information and empower you to pursue informed choices.

4. Routinely Survey and Change: Retirement arranging is a continuous interaction. Consistently audit your monetary arrangement, venture execution, and objectives. As conditions change, for example, economic situations, individual objectives, or well-being contemplations, change your retirement plan in a similar manner.

End:
Exploring retirement arrangements includes cautious thought of monetary elements, embracing the way of life changes, and getting ready for possible difficulties. By evaluating what

is happening, making an exhaustive retirement spending plan, and expanding retirement investment funds, you can guarantee a strong monetary establishment. Adjusting to the way of life changes, keeping up with social associations, and dealing with your time successfully will assist you with Chapter taking in a satisfying retirement. Recognizing expected difficulties, for example, life span, market instability, medical services expenses, and expansion, permits you to proactively address these dangers. Looking for proficient direction, remaining informed, and consistently surveying your retirement plan will offer the help required for a fruitful retirement venture. Keep in mind, every individual's retirement is special, so tailor your arrangement to line up with your objectives, values, and goals. With cautious preparation and smart direction, you can set out on a compensating retirement venture that brings monetary security, individual satisfaction, and inner harmony.

•Investigating retirement accounts and improving retirement pay.

Retirement accounts assume an essential Chapter in building a safe monetary future. By understanding the various kinds of retirement accounts accessible, their advantages and downsides, and carrying out powerful techniques, people can streamline their retirement records to boost pay during their brilliant years. In this paper, we will investigate the best procedures for investigating and advancing retirement records to accomplish this objective.

Sorts of Retirement Records:
1. 401(k) Plans: Presented by businesses, 401(k) plans permit representatives to contribute a Chapter of their compensation on a pre-charge premise. The commitments develop charge conceded until withdrawal. A few managers may likewise offer matching commitments, giving a prompt lift to retirement investment funds.

2. Conventional Individual Retirement Records (IRAs): People can add to a Customary IRA on a pre-charge premise, and the commitments develop a charge conceded. Withdrawals in retirement are dependent upon annual expenses. Commitments might be charge deductible given pay qualification.

3. Roth IRAs: Roth IRAs are supported with after-charge commitments, and qualified withdrawals in retirement are tax-exempt. This record type is reasonable for people who expect to be in a higher duty Chapter in retirement or need to broaden their expense risk.

4. Worked on Worker Annuity (SEP) IRAs: SEP IRAs are intended for independently employed people and entrepreneurs. Commitments are made on a pre-charge premise, and the record develops charges conceded. SEP IRAs offer higher commitment limits than Customary or Roth IRAs.

Techniques for Expanding Pay in Retirement:

1. Begin Early and Contribute Routinely: The force of intensifying works best when you start early and contribute every time to your retirement accounts. Expect to contribute the greatest reasonable sum every year to make the most of tax cuts and potential speculation development.

2. Exploit Business Matches: If your manager offers a matching commitment in your 401(k) plan, contribute in some measure to the point of getting the greatest match. This is free cash that can altogether help your retirement investment funds.

3. Differentiate Your Ventures: Keep an expanded speculation portfolio inside your retirement accounts. Designate your ventures across different resource classes, like stocks, bonds, and worldwide speculations. Broadening oversees risk and possibly increments returns over the long haul.

4. Rebalance Routinely: Intermittently audit and rebalance your retirement portfolio to keep up with your ideal resource assignment. Rebalancing includes selling resources that have performed well and purchasing those that have failed to meet expectations, guaranteeing your portfolio lines up with your gamble resistance and speculation objectives.

5. Think about Roth Changes: If you have a Conventional IRA or 401(k) with pre-charge commitments, you might consider switching some or every last bit of it over completely to a Roth IRA. This methodology can give charge broadening and possibly bring down your future assessment obligation in retirement.

6. Oversee Expenses: Be aware of the charges associated with conclusion, exploring and optimizing retirement accounts is crucial for maximizing income in retirement. By understanding the different types of retirement accounts available, contributing regularly, diversifying investments, implementing effective strategies, and considering risks, individuals can

maximize their income potential. Start early, contribute regularly, diversify investments, and seek professional advice when needed. With careful planning and informed decision-making, you can create a robust retirement plan that provides peace of mind and allows you to enjoy a financially fulfilling retirement journey.

CHAPTER 8

Assessment Enhancement and Abundance Development

Charge enhancement is a vital Chapter of abundance for the executives and can essentially influence long-haul monetary achievement. By figuring out charge regulations, executing compelling techniques, and pursuing informed choices, people can limit their duty risk and amplify their abundance development potential. In this exhaustive aid, we will investigate fundamental subjects and procedures connected with charge improvement and abundance development, giving point-by-point clarifications and useful guidance for perusers to apply to their monetary circumstance.

1. Figuring out Assessment Regulations:

1.1. Charge Chapter Framework: Dive more deeply into the ever-evolving charge Chapter framework to comprehend how duty rates increment as pay levels rise. Know about the minor expense rate and powerful duty rate to decide the effect on your general assessment risk.

1.2. Allowances and Attributes: Investigate accessible derivations and credits to diminish available pay. Models incorporate home loan interest allowances, understudy loan interest derivations, and kid tax breaks. Research qualification rules and make the most of these open doors.

1.3. Capital Increases and Profit Duties: Find out about the different expense rates applied to capital additions and profits, contingent upon the holding time frame and sort of speculation. Consider charging productive speculation systems to limit charges on venture pay.

2. Charge Advancement Systems:

2.1. Retirement Records: Expand commitments to burden advantaged retirement accounts, for example, 401(k)s, Customary IRAs, and Roth IRAs. Comprehend the expense ramifications of each record type and pick the one that lines up with your retirement objectives and assessment methodology.

2.2. Charge Misfortune Reaping: Offset capital increases by selling ventures that have encountered misfortunes. This procedure can decrease your available pay and possibly produce charge reserve funds.

2.3. Altruistic Commitments: Give to qualified magnanimous associations to get charge derivations. Comprehend the standards administering magnanimous commitments and save fitting documentation for charge purposes.

2.4. Wellbeing Bank accounts (HSAs): Add to HSAs if qualified. These records offer triple tax cuts - commitments are charge deductible, development is tax-exempt, and withdrawals for qualified clinical costs are tax-exempt.

2.5. Home Preparation: Carry out compelling domain arranging systems to limit bequest burdens and guarantee the smooth exchange of abundance to people in the future. Work with a home arranging lawyer to lay out wills, trusts, and different instruments that line up with your objectives.

3. Abundance Development Strategies:

3.1. Enhancement: Construct a differentiated speculation portfolio to oversee hazards and catch potential learning experiences. Dispense resources across various resource classes, like stocks, bonds, land, and elective speculations.

3.2. Long haul Effective financial planning: Take on a drawn-out speculation way to deal with the benefit from intensifying returns. Oppose the compulsion to time the market and spotlight on a very organized money growth strategy lined up with your monetary objectives.

3.3. Mitigating risk: Contribute a proper sum routinely, paying little mind to economic situations. This procedure decreases the effect of momentary market vacillations and permits you to purchase more offers when costs are low and fewer offers when costs are high.

3.4. Detached Money management: Consider putting resources into minimal expense file assets or trade exchanged reserves (ETFs) that track wide market lists. Aloof financial planning dispenses with the need to pick individual stocks and expects to match the presentation of the general market.

3.5. Land Ventures: Investigate land as a speculation road. Investment properties, land venture trusts (REITs), and land crowdfunding stages offer open doors for abundance development and potential duty benefits.

4. Viable Guidance for Expense Enhancement and Abundance Development:

4.1. Ordinary Audit and Change: Persistently screen what is happening, charge regulations, and speculation portfolio. Routinely audit and change your assessment advancement and abundance development systems to adjust to changing conditions and make the most of new open doors.

4.2. Look for Proficient Direction: Talk with a certified duty guide or monetary organizer to explore complex expense regulations and foster a customized charge streamlining and abundance development methodology. Experts can give significant experiences, assist with distinguishing charge-saving open doors, and guarantee consistency with guidelines.

4.3. Remain Informed: Keep yourself refreshed on charge regulation changes, venture patterns, and monetary news that might affect your duty advancement and abundance development systems. Remain informed through trustworthy sources, go to workshops or online courses, and take Chapter in consistent learning.

4.4. Track Costs and Keep up with Records: Keep nitty gritty records of pay, costs, ventures, and assessment-related archives. Sort out your monetary data and keep up with legitimate documentation to help derivations, credits, and exchanges.

4.5. Think about Geographic Expense Advancement: If practical, investigate amazing chances to improve your duty circumstance by migrating to regions with ideal assessment regulations, for example, states with no annual assessment or nations with worthwhile assessment frameworks. Notwithstanding, cautiously assess the general effect and potential way of life changes related to such choices.

4.6. Be Aware of Dangers: While charge streamlining and abundance development techniques can give critical advantages, it's vital to know about likely dangers. Comprehend the dangers related to various venture vehicles, look for broadening, and assess the compromises among hazards and possible returns.

End:
Charge streamlining and abundance development are major chapters of long-haul monetary achievement. By grasping duty regulations, executing powerful systems, and settling on informed choices, people can limit charge liabilities, expand speculation returns, and create financial momentum after some time. It is essential to routinely survey and change techniques, look for proficient direction when required, and remain informed about charge regulation changes and monetary patterns. Keep in mind, every individual's monetary circumstance is extraordinary, so fitting expense advancement and abundance development procedures to your Chapter's ocular conditions and goals is fundamental. With cautious preparation, steadiness, and proactive direction, you can upgrade your assessment circumstance and make ready for supported abundance development and monetary thriving.

• Figuring out charges, charge proficient techniques, and records

Charges assume a critical Chapter in our monetary lives, affecting our pay, ventures, and in general riches. In this complete aid, we will dive into the universe of charges, charge-effective techniques, and records. We will investigate how to comprehend charges, the different kinds of duties, methodologies for limiting assessments, the various sorts of records accessible, and how to pick the right record for your circumstance. Furthermore, we will examine the likely advantages of duty-effective systems to assist you with advancing your monetary results.

Area 1: Figuring out Expenses

1.1 What Are Duties?
- Characterize charges as necessary monetary commitments forced by the public authority to finance public consumptions and administrations.

1.2 Sorts of Assessments:

- Annual Assessment: Make sense of how personal expense is determined in light of various duty sections and the ever-evolving charge framework.
- Capital Increases Duty: Examine how capital additions charge is applied to benefits from the offer of resources and separate between the present moment and long haul capital increases.
- Profit Duty: Make sense of how the profit charge is collected on pay received from stocks and different ventures.
- Domain Assessment: Talk about the home duty, which is forced on the exchange of abundance starting with one age and then onto the next.
- Deals Duty: Portray deals charge as a rate added to the cost of labor and products.
- Local charge: Make sense of local charge as a duty exacted on land possessions.
- Different Expenses: Momentarily notice different charges, for example, finance charge, extract assessment, and gift charge.

Segment 2: Limiting Charges

2.1 Expense Allowances and Credits:
- Investigate normal expense allowances, for example, contract revenue, understudy loan revenue, and altruistic commitments.
- Talk about tax breaks, for example, the Kid Tax reduction and the Procured Annual Tax break.

2.2 Duty Arranging Methodologies:
- Amplify Retirement Commitments: Make sense of the advantages of adding to burden advantaged retirement accounts, for example, 401(k)s and IRAs, to bring down available pay.
- Utilize Adaptable Spending Records (FSAs) and Wellbeing Investment accounts (HSAs): Talk about the upsides of these records for diminishing available pay and putting something aside for clinical costs.
- Think about Timing of Pay and Costs: Make sense of how conceding pay or speeding up costs can affect available pay in various fiscal years.
- Charge Misfortune Collecting: Depict the procedure of counterbalancing capital additions

with capital misfortunes to diminish available pay.

- Use Expense Proficient Ventures: Talk about the advantages of putting resources into charge effective vehicles, for example, file assets or duty oversaw reserves.

Area 3: Kinds of Records

3.1 Individual Retirement Records (IRAs):
- Conventional IRAs: Make sense of the expense benefits of adding to a Customary IRA and the duty suggestions upon withdrawal during retirement.
- Roth IRAs: Examine the tax-exempt development and qualified withdrawals of Roth IRA commitments, as well as pay constraints for commitments.
- SEP IRAs and Basic IRAs: Give an outline of these retirement accounts accessible for independently employed people and entrepreneurs.

3.2 Boss-Supported Retirement Records:

- 401(k)s: Examine the advantages of adding to a 401(k), including pre-charge commitments and potential manager matches.
- 403(b)s and 457 Plans: Momentarily notice these retirement accounts accessible to representatives of specific philanthropic associations and administrative substances, individually.

3.3 Wellbeing Bank accounts (HSAs):
- Make sense of the assessment benefits of adding to an HSA and how it tends to be utilized to put something aside for qualified clinical costs.

3.4 Available Investment Funds:
- Talk about the adaptability of available money market funds and how capital additions and profits are burdened.

Area 4: Picking the Right Record

4.1 Surveying Your Monetary Objectives and Requirements:

- Assess retirement objectives, expected charge Chapter in retirement, and qualification for various sorts of retirement accounts.
- Consider liquidity necessities and future clinical costs while settling on well-being investment accounts.
- Survey speculation inclinations and long-haul objectives for available investment funds.

4.2 Assessment Contemplations:
- Dissect your current and projected charge circumstance to decide the tax breaks of different records.
- Consider the likely effect of expense regulation changes and future duty rates.

4.3 Openness and Withdrawal Rules:
- Talk about the availability of assets in various records and any punishments or limitations related to early withdrawals.

Area 5: Advantages of Expense Productive Systems

5.1 Improved Abundance Amassing:

- Make sense of how limiting expenses can prompt more noteworthy venture returns and intensifying development after some time.

5.2 Better Income:
- Talk about how to charge productive methodologies that can let loose more assets for reserve funds and ventures, upgrading by and large income.

5.3 Home Preparation and Abundance Move:
Feature the advantages of duty-productive techniques in bequest arranging, including limiting home assessments and expanding abundance to people in the future.
End:

Grasping duties, utilizing charge-effective techniques, and using the right records are fundamental Chapters of monetary achievement. By grasping various kinds of assessments, carrying out systems to limit burdens, and picking appropriate records, people can streamline their monetary results. Make sure to talk with a certified expense counselor or monetary organizer to fit these methodologies to your Chapter's ocular conditions. By adopting a proactive strategy to burden improvement, you can upgrade abundance development, expand venture returns, and secure a more prosperous monetary future.

CHAPTER 9

Enduring Business sector Instability

Market instability is an inborn piece of effective financial planning. Monetary business sectors are affected by different factors like financial circumstances, international occasions, and financial backer opinion, which can prompt variances in stock costs, security yields, and other resource classes. In this extensive aid, we will investigate methodologies for overseeing and moderating gambling during times of market unpredictability. We will talk about the ongoing economic situations, the potential for market moves, and best practices for risk executives.

Area 1: Figuring out Market Unpredictability

1.1   Characterizing   Business   Sector
Unpredictability:
- Make sense of what market unpredictability is
and the way things are estimated, for example,
using instability files like the VIX.
- Examine the variables that add to advertise
instability, including financial markets, financial
backers' way of behaving, and outer occasions.

1.2 The Effect of Market Unpredictability:
- Investigate what market unpredictability can
mean for venture portfolios, including expected
misfortunes,   expanded   vulnerability,   and
profound pressure.
- Feature the significance of overseeing risk
during   unpredictable   periods   to   protect
long-haul monetary objectives.

Area 2: Economic Situations and Likely Moves

2.1 Current Economic situations:

- Give an outline of the ongoing business sector climate, including late patterns and factors affecting instability.
- Talk about the effect of monetary pointers, corporate profit, and worldwide occasions on market feeling.

2.2 Potential Market Movements:
- Analyze factors that could set off market shifts, for example, changes in loan fees, political turns of events, or changes in buyer conduct.
- Examine how financial backers ought to screen market pointers and remain informed about expected movements to pursue informed venture choices.

Area 3: Prescribed Procedures for Hazard The executives

3.1 Broadening:
- Make sense of the significance of broadening in overseeing risk.
- Talk about how enhancement across resource classes, areas, and geographic districts can assist

with decreasing the effect of market unpredictability.

3.2 Resource Distribution:
- Feature the meaning of vital resource distribution in overseeing risk.
- Examine the advantages of having an even portfolio that lines up with the financial backer's gamble resilience and long-haul objectives.

3.3 Gamble Appraisal and Hazard Resilience:
- Make sense of the significance of evaluating individual gamble resilience and adjusting speculations as needs be.
- Examine risk appraisal devices and philosophies that can assist financial backers with understanding their gamble profile.

3.4 Ordinary Portfolio Survey:
- Underline the requirement for ordinary portfolio surveys to guarantee arrangement with speculation goals and change resilience.
- Examine the advantages of rebalancing portfolios to keep up with wanted resource assignments.

3.5 Minimizing risk:

- Make sense of the idea of minimizing risk over the long haul and how it can alleviate the effect of market unpredictability.

- Examine how standard commitments to venture records can streamline the impacts of market changes.

3.6 Using Stop-Misfortune Orders:

- Examine the utilization of stop-misfortune orders as a gamble on the executive's instrument.

- Make sense of how stop-misfortune orders can assist with restricting possible misfortunes via consequently selling a venture on the off chance that it arrives at a foreordained cost.

3.7 Long Haul Effective financial planning:

- Feature the advantages of a drawn-out speculation approach in overseeing market unpredictability.

- Examine the expected benefits of remaining contributed and keeping away from traditionalist choices in light of momentary market developments.

Segment 4: Close-to-home Administration

4.1 Controlling Profound Reactions:
- Examine the job of feelings in venture navigation.
- Give methodologies for dealing with feelings during times of market unpredictability, for example, keeping fixed on long-haul objectives and staying away from indiscreet activities.

4.2 Looking for Proficient Direction:
- Feature the benefit of talking with a monetary guide during seasons of market instability.
- Examine how monetary counselors can give objective exhortation and assist financial backers with exploring tempestuous business sectors.

End:
Overseeing and alleviating risk during market unpredictability is fundamental for long-haul venture achievement. By understanding economic situations, executing best practices for

the risk of the executives, and keeping a trained methodology, financial backers can explore times of unpredictability with more noteworthy certainty. Recall that market instability presents valuable open doors as well as difficulties, and a very much-built venture system can assist with enduring business sector storms. Remain informed, keep fixed on your drawn-out objectives, and look for proficient direction when expected to capitalize on your venture process.

• Mental viewpoints, sane financial planning, and systems for disturbance.

Contributing isn't exclusively about investigating monetary information and going with informed choices. It is likewise a profoundly mental undertaking, impacted by feelings, inclinations, and insights. In this article, we will investigate the mental Chapters of level headed financial planning and systems for exploring violent business sectors. We will dig into the ramifications of market instability on financial backer feelings, the dangers and compensations of long haul versus momentary speculations, and other significant points. By understanding the mental elements at play and carrying out judicious techniques, financial backers can more readily explore fierce business sectors and accomplish their monetary objectives.

Segment 1: The Effect of Market Unpredictability on Financial Backer Feeling

1.1 Conduct Money:

- Present the field of social money and its importance to financial backers' way of behaving.
- Examine how market instability can set off profound reactions and mental predispositions that influence speculation choices.

1.2 Trepidation and Ravenousness:

- Investigate the job of dread and avarice in driving financial backer opinion during violent business sectors.
- Make sense of how dread can prompt frenzy selling and botched open doors, while covetousness can bring about silly richness and over-the-top gamble-taking.

1.3 Group Mindset:

- Talk about the peculiarity of crowd mindset in effective financial planning and its impact on market unpredictability.
- Make sense of how financial backers frequently follow the group, prompting overstated market developments.

1.4 Defeating Profound Predispositions:

- Give procedures for conquering close-to-home inclinations during tempestuous business sectors, for example, keeping a drawn-out point of view and staying away from imprudent activities.

- Examine the advantages of close-to-home separation and level headed navigation.

Segment 2: Long haul Money management versus Transient Exchanging

2.1 The Enticement of Momentary Exchanging:

- Analyze the appeal of transient exchanging during unstable business sectors.
- Talk about the expected dangers and difficulties related to momentary exchanging, including exchange costs, market timing, and profound pressure.

2.2 The-Examine how a drawn-out approach can moderate the effect of transient market changes and saddle the force of intensifying returns.

2.3 Key Resource Allotment:

- Make sense of the significance of key resource allotment in long-haul effective financial planning.

- Examine how enhancement across resource classes can assist with overseeing risk and streamline returns over the long haul.

2.4 Minimizing risk:

- Investigate the idea of mitigating risk as a procedure for long-haul effective money management.
- Examine how normal commitments to venture portfolios can streamline market instability and possibly upgrade returns.

Segment 3: Normal Methodologies for Exploring Tempestuous Business Sectors

3.1 Central Examination:

- Talk about the significance of crucial examinations in assessing venture potential open doors.
- Make sense of how investigating organization financials, industry patterns, and economic situations can assist financial backers with pursuing normal choices.

3.2 Gamble The board:

- Feature the meaning of chance administration during fierce business sectors.
- Examine systems for differentiating portfolios, setting stop-misfortune arrangements, and overseeing position sizes to moderate likely misfortunes.

3.3 Antagonist Contributing:

- Make sense of the idea of antagonist putting and its significance in violent business sectors.
- Examine how antagonist financial backers make the most of market opinion limits and look for potential open doors where others see just dangers.

3.4 Exploration and A reasonable Level of Effort:

- Stress the significance of careful exploration and an expected level of effort in normal financial planning.

- Examine the job of breaking down fiscal reports, directing industry research, and remaining informed about market improvements.

3.5 Financial Backer Instruction and Constant Learning:

- Talk about the significance of financial backer training and constant learning in objective money management.
- Feature the benefit of remaining refreshed on venture standards, methodologies, and market patterns.

Financial backers must perceive the job of social money in their dynamic cycle. Market instability frequently sets off profound reactions and mental predispositions that can prompt silly speculation choices. Dread and ravenousness become unmistakable elements, affecting financial backers to go with imprudent decisions in light of transient market developments. Beating these close-to-home inclinations requires discipline and an emphasis on long-haul objectives. By keeping a drawn-out point of view, financial backers can keep away from traditionalist choices and profit by speculating open doors that might emerge during market slumps.

Long-haul effective money management has shown to be a strong methodology for enduring fierce business sectors. While momentary exchange might appear to be enticing during unpredictable times, it is critical to consider the potential dangers implied, for example, exchange costs, market timing difficulties, and profound pressure. Then again, long-haul money management permits financial backers to profit from the influence of intensifying returns and tackle the steadiness and development capability of all-around expanded portfolios.

The key resource portion assumes a critical Chapter in long-haul effective financial planning. By broadening speculations across various resource classes, like stocks, bonds, and land, financial backers can spread their gamble and possibly enhance returns. Minimizing risk is one more successful system for long-haul effective financial planning. Ordinary commitments to speculation portfolios assist with streamlining market unpredictability by purchasing more offers when costs are low and fewer offers when costs are high, bringing about a great normal expense over the long run.

In exploring violent business sectors, level headed techniques are fundamental. The essential investigation gives a strong groundwork for assessing speculation's valuable open doors. By directing inside and out research on organization financials, industry patterns, and economic situations, financial backers can go with informed choices given natural worth as opposed to transient market variances. Risk the executives is one more basic Chapter of objective money management. Broadening, setting stop-misfortune orders to restrict expected misfortunes, and overseeing position sizes are successful gamble alleviation methodologies.

Antagonist contribution can likewise be an important technique during unstable business sectors. Antagonist financial backers exploit market feeling limits by conflicting with the crowd mindset. At the point when the market is excessively critical, they look for amazing open doors that others might neglect, possibly profiting from future market recuperations. In any case, it means quite a bit to direct exhaustive exploration and a reasonable level of effort to guarantee that antagonist ventures have areas of strength for an establishment.

Proceeded with financial backer instruction and nonstop learning are essential for remaining informed and pursuing level headed speculation choices. The monetary scene is continually developing, and financial backers need to adjust to changing economic situations. By growing their insight through perusing, going to courses, and drawing in with monetary specialists, financial backers can upgrade how they might interpret venture standards and techniques.

All in all, exploring fierce business sectors requires a blend of judicious reasoning, close-to-home control, and informed direction. Understanding the mental Chapters of effective money management and carrying out sane systems can assist financial backers with enduring business sector unpredictability and make long-haul monetary progress. By monitoring market opinion, perceiving the advantages of long-haul financial planning, and utilizing systems, for example, resource allotment, risk the board, antagonist contributing, and persistent learning, financial backers can explore violent business sectors with certainty and improve their venture results.

CHAPTER 10

The Way to Monetary Autonomy

The fact that many people try to make achieving financial freedom an objective. It is the condition of having adequate abundance and assets to cover everyday costs without depending on business pay. Monetary autonomy gives opportunity, security, and the capacity to seek after one's interests and objectives without monetary limitations. In this complete aid, we will investigate the means one can take to acquire independence from the rat race and security. We will cover methodologies for planning, effective financial planning, and saving, as well as guidance for keeping away from obligation and overseeing funds actually. By following these means, people can leave on the way to monetary autonomy.

Segment 1: Building a Strong Groundwork

1.1 Evaluating Current Monetary Circumstance:
- Direct an intensive assessment of your ongoing monetary standing, including pay, costs, resources, and obligations.
- Recognize regions for development and put forth clear monetary objectives.

1.2 Making a Spending plan:
- Foster a far reaching spending plan that lines up with your monetary objectives.
- Track pay and costs, focus on investment funds, and dispense assets for fundamental requirements and optional spending.

1.3 Overseeing Obligation:
- Figure out the various kinds of obligations and their suggestions.
- Carry out systems to take care of exorbitant interest obligations and keep away from pointless obligation amassing.

1.4 Laying out a Just-in-case account:

- Underline the significance of having a just-in-case account to cover startling costs.
- Set an investment funds target and bit by bit construct an asset that can cover a while of everyday costs.

Segment 2: Saving and Contributing for What's in store

2.1 Putting forth Clear Investment funds Objectives:
- Characterize present moment, mid-term, and long haul investment funds objectives.
- Decide the sum required and the time span for every objective.

2.2 Executing an Investment funds Technique:
- Investigate various reserve funds vehicles, for example, high return investment accounts, authentications of store (Discs), and currency market accounts.
- Robotize reserve funds by setting up programmed moves from your pay to your bank accounts.

2.3 Grasping the Force of Progressive accrual:
- Make sense of the idea of accruing funds and its effect on long haul reserve funds and ventures.
- Support early and steady reserve funds to boost the advantages of self multiplying dividends.

2.4 Money management for Development:
- Present the idea of financial planning and its true capacity for abundance collection.
- Examine different speculation choices, like stocks, securities, shared assets, and land.

2.5 Enhancement and Resource Portion:
- Feature the significance of enhancement in overseeing venture risk.
- Talk about the idea of resource portion and how it helps balance hazard and return.

Segment 3: Fostering an Abundance Mentality and Way of life

3.1 Developing an Abundance Mentality:
- Underscore the significance of embracing a positive and proactive outlook towards abundance creation.
- Examine the job of mentality in accomplishing monetary objectives and defeating obstructions.

3.2 Limiting Way of life Expansion:
- Urge people to stay away from pointless costs and way of life expansion as their pay increases.
- Advance a thrifty mentality and cognizant ways of managing money.

3.3 Boosting Pay Potential:
- Give techniques to expand pay, like chasing after advanced education, procuring new abilities, or beginning a side business.
- Investigate valuable open doors for recurring sources of income, for example, investment properties or profit paying ventures.

3.4 Overseeing and Limiting Expenses:

- Feature the meaning of expense arranging and figuring out the assessment ramifications of different monetary choices.
- Investigate procedures for boosting charge effectiveness, for example, adding to retirement records and exploiting charge derivations.

3.5 Looking for Proficient Direction:
- Suggest looking for the help of monetary counselors or specialists to improve monetary systems and address explicit necessities.
- Feature the significance of continuous schooling and remaining informed about individual accounting and speculation standards.

I'm Rundown,
Acquiring monetary freedom and security requires an efficient methodology and a guarantee to sound monetary practices. By building a strong groundwork, saving and contributing shrewdly, and developing an abundance mentality and way of life, people can show themselves a way to independencc from the rat race. It is fundamental to constantly reevaluate and change monetary plans as

conditions change and to stay restrained and zeroed in on long haul objectives. Through cautious planning, reasonable money management, and key navigation, people can clear their direction toward monetary autonomy, furnishing them with the opportunity and security they want throughout everyday life.

Working out autonomy, procedures, and advantages.

Chasing achievement, creating freedom, making compelling methodologies, and receiving the rewards of these endeavors assume fundamental Chapter s. This article will dive into the meaning of these three components and how they cooperate to assist people with arriving at their objectives. We will investigate instances of how freedom, techniques, and advantages can be outfitted to make progress, while additionally considering the difficulties and valuable open doors that emerge en route.

Area 1: Creating Freedom

1.1 Characterizing Autonomy:
- Make sense of the idea of autonomy and its significance in making progress.
- Examine how autonomy connects with self-improvement, direction, and confidence.

1.2 Developing Autonomy:
- Investigate techniques for creating freedom, like taking responsibility for activities, encouraging self-control, and embracing a development mentality.
- Give instances of people who have developed autonomy and made progress in their separate fields.

1.3 Beating Difficulties:
- Examine the difficulties that might emerge while creating freedom, like apprehension about disappointment, cultural tensions, and self-question.
- Give systems to defeat thesc difficulties, including building an encouraging group of

people, defining sensible objectives, and embracing strength.

Area 2: Creating Successful Procedures

2.1 Figuring out the Significance of Techniques:
- Make sense of why procedures are fundamental for making progress.
- Examine how procedures give a guide to activity, help in beating hindrances, and boost effectiveness.

2.2 Distinguishing Objectives and Targets:
- Examine the most common way of laying out clear objectives and goals as an establishment for making compelling techniques.
- Give instances of how people have characterized their objectives and created procedures to accomplish them.

2.3 Planning Activity Plans:
- Investigate the method involved with planning activity plans given distinguished objectives and targets.

- Examine the significance of separating objectives into more modest, noteworthy stages and focusing on undertakings.

2.4 Adjusting and Repeating:
- Feature the significance of adaptability and flexibility in refining and changing systems given criticism and evolving conditions.
- Give instances of people or associations that have effectively adjusted their methodologies to make long-haul progress.

Area 3: Receiving the Rewards

3.1 Advantages of Autonomy and Procedures:
- Talk about the unmistakable and immaterial advantages that emerge from creating freedom and making successful procedures.
- Models might incorporate individual satisfaction, expanded open doors, monetary steadiness, and further developed thinking skills.

3.2 Observing Achievements and Accomplishments:

- Underscore the significance of perceiving and praising achievements and accomplishments along the way to progress.
- Talk about how these snapshots of festivity can fuel inspiration and move to proceed with progress.

3.3 Supporting Achievement:
- Investigate systems for keeping up with and supporting achievement whenever it is accomplished.
- Talk about the significance of progressing self-awareness, consistent learning, and adjusting to new difficulties and amazing open doors.

End:
Creating autonomy, making viable methodologies, and receiving the rewards of these endeavors are basic chapters of making progress. By encouraging autonomy, people can take responsibility for activities and clear their way toward progress. Making compelling methodologies gives a guide to activity and assists people with exploring difficulties and

boosts the effectiveness. Receiving the rewards of autonomy and procedures, like individual satisfaction and expanded open doors, supports the excursion toward progress. In any case, it is critical to recognize the difficulties and open doors that emerge en route and to move toward them with versatility and flexibility. By grasping the significance of creating autonomy, making viable methodologies, and embracing the advantages, people can situate themselves for long-all outcomes in their proficient undertakings.

CONCLUSION:

Last Contemplations and Support

Recognized visitors, regarded workforce, pleased guardians, and graduates, today denote a groundbreaking event as we accumulate to commend your accomplishments and the start of another Chapter in your lives. As you stand on the cliff of vast potential outcomes, I need to express your last viewpoints and consolation that will move you to embrace the future with energy, reason, and a pledge to have a constructive outcome on the planet. The information and abilities you have gained all through your instructive excursion have furnished you with the devices to make a change, and this is the ideal opportunity to release your true capacity and do great things.

Area 1: Embracing the Force of Potential Outcomes

1.1 A Universe of Boundless Open Doors:

In the present interconnected and quickly impacting the world, the open doors accessible to you are tremendous and various. The force of innovation, globalization, and advancement has opened up new pathways for progress. Embrace these potential open doors and trust in your capacity to explore strange regions, utilizing your schooling and abilities to have a significant effect.

1.2 Embracing Vulnerability:

While vulnerability can be disrupting, it is likewise an entryway to development and revelation. Embrace the obscure with great enthusiasm, for in snapshots of vulnerability genuine leap forwards and self-awareness happen. Consider the trailblazers and visionaries who fashioned new ways despite vulnerabilities and proceeded to impact the world. Be strong, face challenges, and have confidence in your capacities to explore unknown waters.

1.3 Developing Strength:

The way to progress is seldom smooth. Difficulties, misfortunes, and disappointments are inescapable. Yet, it is through flexibility that we track down the solidarity to beat these obstructions. Develop versatility by keeping a positive outlook, looking for help from friends and family, and tutors, and reevaluating disappointments as significant learning opens doors. Keep in mind, not the shortfall of misfortune characterizes achievement, yet the way that you answer it.

Segment 2: Having a Constructive Outcome

2.1 Finding Your Energy:

As you set out on this new period of your life, carve out the opportunity to investigate your interests and adjust them to your professions and life decisions. Track down significance and reason in your undertakings, for it is through enthusiasm that you will track down the inspiration and drive to have an enduring effect. Seek after your inclinations earnestly and let your energy guide your excursion.

2.2 Involving Information and Abilities for Good:

The training you have gotten isn't only for individual increase; it is an amazing asset for making positive change. Consider how your insight and abilities can add to settling worldwide difficulties and working on the existence of others. Whether you decide to handle ecological issues, advance civil rights, or develop in the area of innovation, utilize your schooling to have an effect and leave an enduring heritage.

2.3 Embracing Variety and Incorporation:

In a world that is turning out to be progressively interconnected, variety and consideration are a higher priority than at any time in recent memory. Embrace variety in the entirety of its structures and cultivate comprehensive conditions where everybody's voice is heard and esteemed. Perceive the lavishness of alternate points of view and the potential for aggregate development and development. By supporting variety and incorporation, you will make an additional chapter in the inland amicable world.

2.4 Developing Sympathy and Empathy:

As you explore your own proficient lives, never fail to focus on the force of sympathy and empathy. Put yourself in the shoes of others, look to grasp their encounters, and act with graciousness and sympathy. Little demonstrations of empathy can make waves of positive change that reach out ng way past their nearby effect. Be a power for good in the existence of everyone around you.

Segment 3: Exploring the Excursion Ahead

3.1 Nonstop Learning and Flexibility:

The world is developing at an exceptional speed, and it requires nonstop learning and flexibility to flourish. Focus on long-lasting learning, remain inquisitive, and embrace change. Search out new information, get new abilities, and stay versatile notwithstanding advancing conditions. The capacity to learn, forget, and relearn will be a vital determinant of your future achievement.

3.2 Structure Solid Connections:

No excursion to progress is finished without the help of others. Fabricate solid connections and organizations, both and expertly. Encircle yourself with individuals who elevate and rouse you, who challenge and widen your points of view. Joint effort and cooperation are impetuses for groundbreaking accomplishments. Together, we can accomplish more than we at any point could alone.

3.3 Adjusting Desire and Prosperity:

As you seek after your objectives and yearnings, make sure to focus on your prosperity. Achievement shouldn't come to the detriment of your physical and emotional well-being. Track down a harmony between ambition and self-care. Take time to recharge, nurture your relationships, and engage in activities that bring you joy. A healthy work-life balance will sustain you on your journey towards success.

ConclusionAs you stand here today, outfitted with information, abilities, and a deep longing to have an effect, recollect that what's to come is yours to shape. Embrace the force of conceivable outcomes and let your energy and reason guide you. Utilize your schooling for individual increase, yet in addition as an impetus for positive change. Be intense, tough, and humane as you explore the excursion ahead. Recall that achievement isn't characterized exclusively by private accomplishments, but by the effect you have on others and the world. Be problem solvers, pioneers in your fields, and supporters of equity and uniformity. As you step into the world with certainty and assurance, know that your place of graduation stands gladly behind you, prepared to praise your victories and back you in your difficulties. Congrats, graduates, and may your prospects be loaded up with vast open doors and the satisfaction that comes from having a constructive outcome on the planet.

•Key important points and support for the excursion to abundance.

The fact that many seek to make the present speedy and steadily impacting the world, accomplishing monetary achievement an objective. Whether you long for independence from the rat race, an agreeable retirement, or the capacity to seek after your interests without stressing over cash, everything starts with dominating the essentials of an individual budget. In this extensive aid, we will investigate the critical illustrations and ways to make monetary progress. From defining and arriving at monetary objectives to making wise ventures and overseeing cash mindfully, we will furnish you with the information and systems to clear your way toward thriving.

Area 1: Defining and Arriving at Monetary Objectives

1.1 Characterizing Your Monetary Objectives:
The most vital move towards monetary achievement is to lay out clear and explicit objectives. Figure out what you need to accomplish monetarily, whether it's taking care of obligations, putting something aside for an initial investment in a house, or building retirement savings. By characterizing your objectives, you make a guide for your monetary excursion.

1.2 Making a Practical Spending Plan:

A financial plan is an amazing asset that empowers you to distribute your pay toward your objectives and costs. Track your pay and costs, focus on your spending, and guarantee that you live within your means. By making a practical spending plan and adhering to it, you deal with your funds and gain ground toward your objectives.

1.3 Saving and Effective money management:
Saving and contributing are vital Chapters of monetary achievement. Construct a backup stash to shield yourself from unexpected costs and plan to save a level of your pay every month. Investigate different speculation choices, like stocks, securities, and shared assets, to develop your abundance after some time. The key is to begin early and be steady in your saving and venture propensities.

Segment 2: Making Wise Ventures

2.1 Figuring out Chance and Return:
Contributing implies facing challenges, yet understanding the connection between hazard

and return is fundamental. Higher-risk ventures might yield more significant yields, however, they likewise accompany more noteworthy unpredictability and possible misfortunes. Broaden your portfolio to alleviate chance and equilibrium ventures across various resource classes.

2.2 Exploration and A reasonable Level of Investment:
Effective money management leads to exhaustive exploration and a reasonable level of effort. Figure out the basics of the venture, assess its likely dangers and rewards, and consider the history of the organization or resource. Try not to go with hasty venture choices given momentary market changes.

2.3 Look for Proficient Exhortation:
If you are new to money management or feel overpowered by the intricacy of the monetary business sectors, think about looking for counsel from a certified monetary consultant. An expert can assist you with examining your monetary

objectives, evaluating your gamble resilience, and fostering a customized venture system.

Segment 3:Planning and Overseeing Cash Mindfully

3.1 Following Costs:
To deal with your cash really, following your expenses is fundamental. Use planning devices or applications to screen your ways of managing money and recognize regions where you can adapt. By monitoring your costs, you can settle on informed choices and focus on your monetary objectives.

3.2 Limiting Obligation:
Obligation can thwart your monetary advancement, so it's pivotal to admirably oversee it. Focus on taking care of exorbitant interest obligations, for example, Visas, and think about obligation combination methodologies if essential. Try not to collect pointless obligations and use credit dependably.

3.3 Living Beneath Your Means:

While it may very well be enticing to surrender to the way of life expansion, living underneath your means is a critical rule of monetary achievement. Separate among needs and needs, practice careful spending, and keep away from superfluous lavish expenditures. By reliably spending short of what you procure, you set out the freedom to save and contribute to what's in store.

Segment 4: Creating Monetary Proficiency and Persistent Learning

4.1 Instructing Yourself:
Monetary achievement requires a strong groundwork of monetary proficiency. Step up to the plate and instruct yourself about individual accounting points, for example, planning, money management, assessments, and retirement arranging. There are various books, digital broadcasts, and online assets accessible to upgrade your monetary information.

4.2 Remaining Informed:

Keep awake to date with monetary patterns, market advancements, and changes in monetary guidelines. The monetary scene is consistently developing, and remaining informed empowers you to go with informed choices and adjust your monetary system likewise.

4.3 Looking for Amazing open doors for Development:
Ceaselessly look for valuable chances to develop your pay and extend your monetary capacities. Think about extra kinds of revenue, investigate pioneering tries, or put resources into your expert improvement to expand your acquiring likely over the long run.
End:

Making monetary progress is an excursion that requires discipline, persistence, and a guard-g-lasting learning. By defining clear monetary objectives, making wise ventures, and dealing with your cash mindfully, you can prepare for a prosperous future. Make sure to embrace the force of compounding, remain fixed on your drawn-out objectives, and be versatile to changes in the monetary scene. Eventually, the very achievement isn't just about gathering abundance but about accomplishing independence from the rat race, security, and the capacity to carry on with a satisfying life. Begin making strides today toward your monetary achievement, and the prizes will be worth the work.